OBJECT
AND IDEA

An Art Critic's Journal 1961-1967

by BRIAN O'DOHERTY

SIMON AND SCHUSTER · NEW YORK

FIRST PRINTING

LIBRARY OF CONGRESS CATALOG CARD NUMBER: 67–20794
DESIGNED BY EVE METZ
MANUFACTURED IN THE UNITED STATES OF AMERICA
BY AMERICAN BOOK–STRATFORD PRESS, INC.

We are particularly grateful to The New York Times for permission to reprint the many pieces which first appeared in its pages, and which are copyright © 1961, 1962, 1963, 1964 by The New York Times Company.

We wish also to thank the following publishers for permission to reprint the pieces attributed to them in this volume: to Newsweek, for pieces copyright © 1964, 1965 by Newsweek, Inc.; to Art and Artists for pieces reprinted from the issues of September, October, November, December 1966 and January 1967; to Art in America for "Hyman Bloom" and "Maxim Karolik," reprinted from No. 3, 1961, and No. 4, 1962, respectively; to Arts Magazine for "Budd Hopkins" which appeared in Volume 40, No. 6, April 1966; to Book Week for "Mapping Our Camp Sites," copyright © 1965 by Book Week, World Journal Tribune, Inc.; to the St. Louis Post-Dispatch for the piece now titled "Boredom and the Amiable Android"; to Life Magazine for "Huntington Hartford: His Book"; and to Studies for "Patrick Collins, Dubliner."

FOR
MARTHA AND BARBARA O'DOHERTY

CONTENTS

INTRODUCTION

In 1961, when I first came to New York—and to *The New York Times*—the scene was very black-and-white, at least on the surface. The Abstract-Expressionist monolith was just beginning to break up. The newer artists had not yet made their formal appearance. In 1962 the Pop artists, vigorously welcomed by the media their work adapted, shattered the monolith. The art world in New York was, for the first time since the avant-garde of the forties appeared, divided. Subsequent years saw that split multiply.

Each year brought a new movement to the surface. In 1963–64 Pop was succeeded—or joined—by Optical art. In 1964–65 it was Object art, which developed into something denoted by titles such as Minimal art and Primary Structures. Each of these titles—Pop, Optical, Object art—covers a number of tendencies with more or less well-defined differences. Similarly such "movements" as Kinetic art, "soft" sculpture and "synesthetic" art had a concurrent development, though one must point out that movements seem often to be confused with categories.

The stimulation of the period was from the rapid development of "new" styles and from the re-examination of criteria which these inventions imposed. The responsibility was to discriminate within the new, not simply to accept or reject it. When confronted with the new there are two main possibilities. One is to attempt to view it in a frame of reference to which the work itself mainly contributes—it is often as difficult to construct the frame of reference as it

9

is to see the work itself. The other is to relate it to similar phenomena in the past, pointing out similarities and precedents. This is often a pretty unfruitful form of conservatism, since similar objects may be produced from entirely different attitudes—or similar attitudes can result in widely different end products. I think one has to forget the past as frequently as one remembers it. Otherwise the acute sense of current art as a phenomenon of the present moment is lost. The present becomes just the current unrolling of the past— not a very useful perspective from which to see new art.

The pieces written between 1961 and 1964—when I was a critic for *The New York Times*—are very much in the nature of a foot soldier's report from the front. Most pieces were, in the usual journalistic practice, written in a few hours and printed immediately. A problem had to be stated, argued and solved within a short space. I don't think this is a bad discipline. It sharpens responses, clarifies ideas and means of expression. (It also invites its own kind of cop-out, which includes the rhetorical screen that keeps a problem out and the indulgence in an irritation which hasn't had time to settle.) I think that some conclusion, some commitment, must be attempted, although I feel conclusions are not very important. Chances must be taken, mistakes made. It's the way you make them that matters. The desire to be right is very bourgeois. Even so, with my present hindsight, it is hard for me to accept my lack of foresight on occasion.

Reading over this book, there are judgments I would change if I were writing it again; there are ideas I would change, and indeed words I would change. But apart from allowing myself the luxury of a more useful word here and there, dropping some superfluous sentences, restoring parts cut by the necessities of newspaper space, and occasionally running two articles on the same subject together, nothing has been changed. For whatever value this book has is mostly in its immediate response to a rapidly changing scene.

A set theory of criticism is, I feel, an academic luxury when working in the journalistic medium, since it becomes a barrier rather than an aid to perception. Catholicity of response is, I would think, obligatory. A prejudice against broad areas of art should disqualify a newspaper critic. Nor do I feel that a newspaper is the place to advance or to condemn a movement. In newspaper criticism, certainly, artists are much more important than movements. Unfortunately, support or otherwise of an individual artist is often interpreted as taking a position on the movement or social group to which he belongs. In all this—and it is so obvious as to be obscure— a certain degree of empiricism is important in preserving openness of response.

Personal taste is, I feel, relatively unimportant, except perhaps in a negative way. Frequently the problem is to construct a just response to what is sometimes opposed to one's taste. Frequently the art that proves most durable is opposed to one's taste, art that—to turn taste into a literal metaphor—forces one to masticate it. Here the current word, and a good one, associated with quality is "toughness"—a sort of built-in resistance to easy solutions and indulgences. "Taste" is, I suppose, most directly about the elegant and the beautiful. The best art in the period 1961–67 has been that which acts against its own taste and finds some effective counterthrust to it.

Empiricism leads one into inconsistencies and contradictions, and the attempt to achieve or maintain consistency is an attempt at a false synthesis. Inconsistencies arise from different frames of reference when approaching a problem. Instead of seeking a common denominator one should be examining the frames of reference in an attempt to establish some sort of relational structure. This, of course, cannot be done under the temporal and spatial limitations of a newspaper situation.

The criticism since 1964 was written primarily for monthly magazines for which one writes in a more leisurely fashion of things one wishes to write about. I don't know how one can continue writing newspaper criticism to any real standard longer than, at the most, five years. Perhaps some enlightened newspaper may introduce the idea of critical sabbaticals.

Frames of reference lead one—as indeed writing any sort of criticism tends to do—into an examination of the critical process. (There is an increasing tendency for criticism to be about criticism rather than about art. Critical self-consciousness is essential, but criticial narcissism often replaces it.) Absolute standards are obsolete. "Psychological" criticism is limited, "formal" criticism a highly useful device that has, however, been discredited by the formal critics. Art criticism has to be reinvented for every generation, and it seems to me that the mode most suitable to dealing with art now is some modification of the "structuralist" criticism that is well established in anthropology and literature. Such multiple frames of reference catch the art object in transit through a section of time in a way impossible for modes that depend completely on the fiction of "development," which is really a critical disguise for the illusion of progress.

Thus the critic should, I feel, be free in his eclecticism, free to choose the conventions within which he should operate—to favor and make judicious investments in rhetorical exposition, arbitrary "sets," stylistic emphasis, to be polemical, to choose and unchoose the present the artist points to. All this leads to an acute awareness of the process by which art is codified, which is far from historical inevitability. It leads away from pure value judgments which seem to me to be less and less important. The nineteenth-century critical eye is mutated to a sort of multifaceted insectual organ which "fixes" a work in a sort of conceptual labyrinth.

Division of occasional criticism over a period of time into categories is a tricky process, since it fixes the criticism, by the very nature of a book, into one pattern. I have chosen one which is a simple mixture of themes and chronology. The first part, "Artists," is subdivided into four sections: "The Modern Tradition"; artists currently "Outside the Mainstream"; "The Last Avant-Garde"— essentially what the heroic generation of the late forties and early fifties was in America;* and "The New Makers," who have more or less come to terms with the social structure and who function within it comfortably enough. The second part, "Patrons and Museums," deals with an essential wing of the "scene." The final part, "Themes and Futures," deals essentially with the stress placed on old values by new objects, and the attempts to find serviceable modes of criticism to deal with them.

I am acutely aware of the split that fundamentally divides the art world now—between those who believe that art has to do with art (not art for art's sake) and those who believe that art has primarily something to do with life. Both imply completely antagonistic views of the nature of time, the nature of art, and the nature of life. Though one can tie this division to historical oppositions such as Poussinistes and Rubénistes, Delacroix versus Ingres, etc., it is a pattern that divides many other fields, e.g., in psychology, Maslow versus Skinner, in law, Kelsen versus Austin. The philosophical roots of such a division are obvious. But I feel that it has less to do with intellectual conviction than with an almost genetic antagonism of seed to seed. The art-as-art view is, of course, always historically triumphant in that art continually survives its contexts and thus its initial "meaning." It is against this art-life dilemma that artists and critics tend to define themselves. The very separation itself has meant cultivation of extremes of ordered preciousness and anarchic disorder, which by parodying the dilemma tend to remove it. Life as a substitute for art and art as a substitute for life (and indeed for art) are now commonplaces. Though the attitudes to the interaction of life and art may be read as corrections of previous attitudes,

* By now we should be able to speak of a closed historical episode, the "modernist" or avant-garde period from Baudelaire to the Abstract Expressionists, from around 1840 to around 1960.

and are thus passing conventions, they demand attention. This book does not investigate them, however, but illustrates in the space of a few years a few moves from art in relation to life toward art in relation to art. It is, curiously, a problem that is more intrinsic to the visual arts than to any other.

PART ONE
ARTISTS

1. THE MODERN TRADITION

Julio Gonzales

As THIS century progresses, some figures from the first half of it, such as Julio Gonzales, are quietly assuming a position of authority and importance. Although it is only twenty years since he died, that brief historical perspective has put his work in the mainstream of modern sculpture.

Gonzales, who died in Paris in a bad year, 1942, already has been mildly deified by those sculptors whose skeletal constructions have stabbed and delineated space for the last two decades. At the Gallery Chalette a large exhibition of Gonzales' work, mounted in aseptic purity, has just opened.

Gonzales was a highly intelligent and thoughtful man whose progress through life was eroded by doubt and difficulty. He went to Paris from Spain in 1900, the same year as Picasso, with whom he was friendly off and on until their collaboration around 1930 finally brought them together. At that time he helped Picasso with his welded sculpture. This moment was a turning point in Gonzales' art.

Before then he had appeared a somewhat shadowy figure on the Parisian scene, present but isolated, aware but uninvolved, although his work showed a certain interest in cubism, and he had discovered a method of cutting a metal sheet and bending parts of it out from the surface to give the effect of constructing or drawing on air.

After the Picasso meeting, Gonzales' Cubist work made a brilliant postscript to that movement's small body of valuable sculpture. Always a physiognomist, he did a series of stunning heads of great formal vitality. And in the mid-thirties he created the series of amputated heads in which the resting lumps of metal are invaded by cubic volumes and hints of features and faces, both united to form metallic human crystals.

His historical importance lies more in those linear sculptures that he brought to perfection in the thirties. They clarified the syntax of a whole phase of modern sculpture and made it easily accessible to those who followed—a generation that includes David Smith and Reg Butler. Gonzales' linear sculptures hold space firmly and seem to define it like geometric projections.

His more solid abstract pieces have a weighty sense of ponderous balance and an unassailable conviction. His sculpture, always based on some representational idea, has certain correspondences to Picasso's paintings of the thirties, and like Picasso's, they are pioneer works.

During his last years, in occupied Paris, Gonzales was forced by war shortages to give up welding and take up modeling again. The head of the screaming woman done the year he died, and cast after his death, freezes an expression of terror in bronze as if he wanted to examine it and perhaps come closer to understanding the anguish around him. It has the same static curiosity as his historic researches into space, the space that, as he said himself, he wanted "to utilize . . . and to construct with . . . as though one were dealing with a newly acquired material." He was.

October 1961
The New York Times

Jan Müller (1923–1958)

THE TRAVAIL and in many ways the triumph of Jan Müller may be seen at the Guggenheim's large retrospective. Müller, who was born in Hamburg, arrived in this country in 1941 after a stormy passage in time of war. In 1950 he began to assert the individuality that finally brought him to vast colorful canvases painted with a deep and clumsy intensity. They show his preoccupation with an otherworld illuminating this one with its deaths and resurrections. Müller died in 1958 in his thirty-sixth year, an age that has been fatal to many brilliant young men. He has received a great deal of attention, especially since his death. This exhibition helps put his work in perspective.

Walking up the winding ramp of the Guggenheim it is possible to ascend through his last crucial eight years. The checkerboard paintings of 1950 begin the exhibition, and they put his color sense, always his greatest strength, through a rigorous discipline. Gradually, in 1953, he introduced figures into this mosaic pattern, figures so tattooed into the color that finding them is a little like waiting for the appearance of an after-image. The big "Adam and Eve" painted the same year is a prophetic picture in its subject matter, in its softly blazing landscape, and in the affecting clumsiness of the large figures.

In 1955–56 he worked on a series of figure paintings in which he tested motifs, or, more probably, discovered them. He also did a number of magically bright landscapes, vibrating with luminous green, that are a little reminiscent of Gauguin's brilliant patterns. Indeed, Müller remained a pattern-maker, for the depth in his pictures, which always lack the sky, is suggested by variations in stroke and in the size of the figures.

In 1956 he came into his own, and his imagination, stimulated by perilous health, began to find a resonance for the ceremony of mortality in literary themes. The Witches' Sabbath from *Faust* is portrayed through a powerful inbreeding of Nolde and Ensor; a painting of Hamlet with the Gravedigger shows more exactly than any other picture where his power and his preoccupations lay. Gradually one can witness the dying of his anguish into larger themes such as the "Temptation of Saint Anthony."

In all these works the paint is handled more thinly, the color is broader and firmer, with clearer contrasts, and the structure of each body is simplified further through the radiance of its color. The patterning and composition become more complex and yet more lucid. So much so, in fact, that the last pictures carry all the way across the vast well of space in the Guggenheim. At times they carry too clearly and the pattern is oversimplified, as in "Concert of Angels."

By this time he had worked into his own individual world, and his last two years, 1956 to 1958, were his best. A number of motifs appear so persistently that they hint at deeper meanings: the horse and rider; the figures standing or sitting on other figures which they occasionally bestride; figures, arms outstretched like Superman, that flash like lightning into the picture; and most persistent of all, the vivid faces that look like Halloween masks. These faces, with multicolored cheek spots like clowns, grimace terribly or present their full faces sightlessly and with obsessive persistence—one never sees a profile. These bulbous elementary faces refer the eye to the similar rotundity of the breasts, like a pathetic and conscious pun. In all these late pictures, as with much northern Gothic art, the themes of sensuality and death run powerfully together.

Müller's present reputation is derived in part from his tragic life and early death. Also, in a decade that rejected the literal image for the inchoate energy of creation, he persistently developed an oeuvre that expressed meditations on mortality and fate by means of a genuine and contemporary expressionism. Since the pressures operating against the creation of a personal vision are immense in today's world, this fact alone gives him some historical importance.

But perhaps his most positive contribution was to make his expressionism constructive, and to keep his basic perspectives clear. His work is that of a man who looked steadily into the pit but did not fall in.

January 1962
The New York Times

Rico Lebrun's Inferno

DANTE was a tough guy. As his circles of hell descended, the invention of images to express anguish and hopelessness increased. To give one example from Canto 28 (translated by the late Dorothy L. Sayers, who also invented some pretty impressive things of her own), Dante saw a torso " . . . split as by a cleaver/His tripes hung by his heels; the pluck and spleen/Showed with the liver and the sordid sack/That turns to dung the food it swallows in."

This is strong stuff. Dante's visions of extreme bestiality occur, however, in a metaphysical netherworld. The physical tortures are surrounded by a halo of fire and ice. Also they are part of a grand design in the poem and in life, based on the certainty of heaven and hell, good and evil.

Rico Lebrun's drawings for the Inferno at the Nordness Gallery are born out of a similar sense of proportion. His writhing horrors are fixed within a great calm, a certainty that tortures may destroy men, but not man. If he had a tendency before to drown in disasters, these illustrations are his resurrection.

Typically, his drawings get down to the lower circles of Dante's hell, as if the deeper the degradation, the more precious the diamond of human dignity to be found there. The talking headless body, the figures in flames and ice, the field of human stumps and

21

bushes, all are called up from an inky deep, abruptly snapshot from an infinite dark. The figures crouch and stretch against the narrow frame, as if encoffined alive.

Like monumental snapshots, Lebrun's figures seem to be caught in evolution from the past, signaling their future. This is most acutely seen in the thieves' punishment in Canto 25, men turning into snakes with a slow, glutinous movement that seems the essence of metamorphosis.

The technique is in itself a drama. The outline is often harshly pushed along; the internal scribble is most often a fascinating form of foreplay—rhythms are sought until the right few lines groove themselves unerringly into descriptive eloquence; the eclipses of the dark wash are often sudden and savage.

Yet there is considerable sensitivity. Gray washes slide over the paper, and, from the glowing white ground, light blooms gently up. The light suggests, hides and reveals, like a theatrical virtuoso. The control of light is the common denominator to all the action.

Thus many of the forms are so masked by light and shadow that they have a mountainous impact. After that they have to be identified and read as figures. But the reading augments the formal impact, like reading a story under a strong headline. At times a few forms run and fuse into a living agglomeration of flesh, a creature greater than the sum of the individual parts that, with recognition, are slowly born from the mother shape. It is a beautifully instinctive demonstration of the unity of form and content in the Michelangelesque tradition.

Lebrun has developed a sort of construction that parallels the human form in a most interesting way. Often headless, armless, with legs amputated to stumps, it is fundamentally a block of torso crisscrossed with lines that bind it tensely. The interesting thing is that the bulges and distortions, like a mirror at a fun fair, reflect the normal. Distortions, after all, mean nothing unless we know the norm that they distort. That standard must necessarily be in our minds.

It seems to be very much in Lebrun's. Thus his work stands very directly in a great (and dangerous) European tradition, from Michelangelo to Rubens and the Baroque, in which the body is the expression of states of mind, a visible intellectual gesture, a living metaphor.*

Speaking of metaphor and image, Lebrun has obviously contemplated his Dante well. His imagination focuses on an image—"So from the broken splint came words and blood/At once" (Canto 13)—and seeks out the common root of metaphor for his own visual recreation. Disregarding a few pale failures in the current show, he succeeds splendidly.

These drawings are not in any way strained. The anguish has become less personal, the psychological distance from disaster has increased, and in that distance lies the power of compassion to be a constructive and not an eroding emotion. Lebrun has gained some of the vision of Dante's Olympian eye. The terrors are still oppressive. But they attend the resurrection of hope from despair.

October 1962
The New York Times

Light on a Dark Horse: Man Ray

WE WERE waiting for Man Ray. A telephone call announced he was imminent. The elevator whirred smoothly up and stopped. The door slid open. Like a Jack emerging from his box, out shot Man Ray into Cordier & Ekstrom's, trailing history behind him. He volleyed around the walls looking at his creations. Then, opening his palms like a Frenchman, he turned to Arne

* Though one contemporary artist calls work in this tradition "Mickey-Mousing," I like the manner.

Ekstrom. "Let me congratulate you on the show." The latter-day
Philadelphia revolutionary was back in town.

"People say I'm a legend," he said a moment later, sitting on, or
rather forming an obviously temporary relationship with, his chair.
"Therefore they think I'm not around any more." By this he meant
demised.

Man Ray, who lives in his chosen city, Paris, couldn't be more
alive. A smallish, vivid man, he moves quickly, thinks quickly, and
gives the answers before the questions, as befits a man who says, "I
have no problems, I have only solutions." One's role was obviously
to be Boswell, not Mike Wallace.

Accompanied wherever he goes by his legend, Man Ray is, of
course, living history—a leading survivor, along with Marcel
Duchamp and Max Ernst, of the eruption known as Dada in its
larval stage, and as Surrealism in its final phase. He went to Paris in
1921, was blown back as far as Los Angeles by the winds of war,
and, as soon as he could, was off to Paris again. He has just written a
book called *Self-Portrait* (Atlantic Monthly Press–Little, Brown), is
painting furiously, and is still irrepressible at seventy-three.

This last statistic is quite incredible. Man Ray doesn't just look
twenty or thirty years younger (he was photographed with Ava
Gardner in 1950 and looked like the male lead); he looks as if age
were irrelevant to him. His hair, which now grows one gray to two
black, is combed onto his forehead in a Roman cut. His face is
intense, his eyes are restless. He wore a white shirt, a bootlace tie,
turned-up cuffs on his sleeves and none on his pants. As we sat in a
corner of the gallery, the chill air of a wet day pressing on the
window behind us, we could see one of his recent paintings, a triple
pun in which a nude girl becomes a leering face that slips into being
a heart now and then.

"I love puns," he said. "That's a plastic pun. I love the play on
words. It's snickered at by most people over here, but in Europe
they're not upset by puns and anagrams and so-called superficial
literary exercises. I like contradictions. We have never attained the

infinite variety and contradiction that exists in nature. Tomorrow I shall contradict myself. That is one way I have of asserting my liberty, the real liberty which one does not find as a member of society.

"There are no two things alike in my work," he said. "That is one way of avoiding boredom—everything has to be different. I couldn't bear to be a Vlaminck or a Renoir. I never paint because I am a painter. I paint because I have an idea. I let the idea recur and recur. It has to haunt me until I have to put it down in concrete form."

Since he creates from ideas, some critics have called Man Ray not a painter but a performer in a circus of ideas, which irritates Man Ray very much.

"How are these performances?" he said, waving a hand at the gallery walls. "I don't want to be called a performer, a trickster. I used to call some of my paintings inventions. Critics talk about my 'being more concerned with novelty than with profundity.' I say that the critic makes a false assumption there. If I spit on a canvas, it's profound, because if it's in me, whatever I do will be profound.

"I don't like the word profound anyway, or the word serious—everything is serious. Or the word modern. 'You're ahead of your time,' I was told. The fact is I was in my time. You were behind it."

He began to play with his famous 1923 "Object to Be Destroyed," a metronome that moved an attached eye back and forth. "In my 1957 retrospective in Paris a bunch of students destroyed it. They were arrested but they said they were only following the title. The insurance company brought me another metronome so I could make another 'Object,' but I said, 'When a painting is destroyed you don't replace it with paints and brushes.' They paid the insurance. Then I made some more. Now I call it 'Indestructible Object.' It's a pity we can't make duplicates of our paintings—you can't destroy a book or a musical score, there are copies."

This wish for permanence seemed most un-Dada-like. Man Ray

was asked about Dada and destruction. "Dada wasn't destruction. Dada wasn't anarchy," he said. "It was a way of expressing anger."

He had some anger to express himself on the function of art critics. "I'm against adverse criticism," he said, joining the great throng of the artistically wronged. "Either you accept the art or you ignore it. It's unethical to condemn it. The artist is just as intelligent and conscious as his critic. I myself have—" he paused—"reactions [to works of art], but I'm very careful, I don't want to jeopardize—anyway if I objected, then I'd have to object to businessmen, the crass products of the market . . . " He waved a hand, materializing vistas of banality.

Since Man Ray was so vehement about critics, the other member of the eternal triangle, the dealer, was mentioned. "My job is to produce," said Man Ray briskly. "Their job is to sell. If they don't do that, I've no use for them." In an access of charity, he added, "They get a thrill out of selling, as I do out of making the pictures."

We spoke of his pioneering rayographs and his classic Surrealist films, including *Les Mystères du Château de De.* "There were lots of film offers after these," said Man Ray. "I wasn't interested in doing more films. I'm trying to do a one-man job, something that leaves me free. It's the only thing that's left to us in present-day society."

May 1963
The New York Times

On the Strange Case of Francis Bacon

THE EXTRAORDINARY THING about the Francis Bacon retrospective at the Guggenheim Museum is its demonstration of how to be a great psychological figure painter in a time that makes it impossible. Behind the devastating success, each painting is a cunning subversion of the time through a limited but brilliant strategy.

The odds against this operation's being successful are considerable. Bacon's surgery is so radical that it is extremely perilous. His subject matter (atrocity, anguish, perversion) has been devalued to cliché. He is not a natural painter and a case could be made as to how badly he often paints. Finally, he seems doubtful of the value of painting, which is at best "a game."

Yet he has produced images that corrupt the imagination and ennoble it, that attack life and preserve it, that devastate and elevate, cutting us between these opposites like a scissors, so that, like the artist, we become both patient and surgeon, victim and assassin, at the same time.

This paradox of Bacon's art is of vital importance for all of us. The more he extends the depth of possible degradation, the more voracious his appetite to spiritualize it. Our particular time has forced on us a consciousness of human action without providing a way to cope with these revelations. Bacon's art does.

It adds the perverse and atrocious to human nature, where they belong, and does it totally without moral judgment. Whoever smartly rejects Bacon's art as a profound expression of aspects of this particular time—as some are beginning to do—just hasn't seen the things the twentieth century keeps under the chromium-plated counter: a body in vivisection, a cancer split open, a mind carefully mutilated, the results of sex murder.

What Bacon does to the human figure is quite clear in a literal way. The figure is filleted to a jellylike blob that can bulge and ripple into any protoplasmic travesty. His people show a curious interaction between structure and movement—ambiguities of movement are suggested by ambiguities of structure, and occasionally vice versa. The norm of the human figure that we all carry in our heads is displaced by a number of possibilities, as if we were watching some game of embryological Russian roulette. (The embryological image can be a useful one in discussing Bacon, some of whose work looks like the contents of the dermoid cyst that sidetracks a human being into a hairy pouch of loose teeth and slime.) Similarly, his emphasis on the perverse seems related to some implied norm of behavior.

The effect is the old one of holding a mirror up to nature to reflect a creature we can examine with some sensual repugnancy before it dawns on us we are looking at ourselves—or some image of our isolation, our sentient brutishness, the unadorned and perilous fact of our existence. Thus the immense concentration of his images, a power frequently inexplicable when one examines the rather obvious structure of his pictures and the fundamental pessimism of his statements.

Bacon is on record as saying that "man now realizes that he is an accident, that he is a completely futile being, that he has to play out the game without reason." The pitiful creature he presents in metamorphosis is an image of the futile anti-hero changing shape, like a slug, to accommodate different stimuli. Pinned against their bright clinical backgrounds, Bacon's hulks are trapped by their necessity to continue living, as he in turn is trapped by his necessity to paint them. And since he seems to think that they and the business of painting them are meaningless, painting becomes a sort of grudging, existential act.

Perhaps the fundamental puzzle about Bacon is how he achieves his perverse nobility and a sort of high art from such a negative basis. Basically, his work is bestiality formalized into a mystique that makes degradation metaphysical, a private Black Mass. Thus his huge "Painting" of 1952 becomes a sort of meaty cathedral, the baroque draperies made of flesh, the anguish stabilized into a ceremonial hysteria.

His people are usually raised on a dais, a throne, a chair, a divan, frequently surrounded by an electric diagram of space (like the skeleton of a cube), isolated against lurid backgrounds of solid color over which black window shades are occasionally pulled down.

These charged spatial environments make anguish bearable in much the same way that ritual does, and they seem located halfway between the theater and the operating room. Within this environment it is eerie to watch snaillike trails of paint crawl and drag across the figures like metaphors for living flesh. The sense of ceremony is inescapable.

Here one can put Bacon into historical perspective without running to Grünewald or Bosch, which is not where he belongs at all. He is the first major expression in paint of a sensibility that runs from de Sade through Rimbaud to Artaud and Genet, and includes such a modern semi-masterpiece as John Osborne's *Under Plain Cover*, with its netherworld of diaphragms and syringes. The best comparison is with Genet. Like him, Bacon is attached to a style of ceremonious presentation that allows him to extend the definition of life to include the underworld of rape, suicide and murder. Again as with Genet, they are not the objects of disgust but of a spiritual passion.

His connection with the history of art he makes clear enough, and one of the scholarly parlor games is going to be the identification of where he got this and that. He got his images from art, photographs and film. He rummages the past looking for the image he can subject to crisis—Velasquez' "Innocent X," Blake's "Ancient of Days," the screaming woman of the Odessa steps sequence in Eisenstein's *Potemkin*. Those pioneers of creative anguish and creative spiritualism, Van Gogh and William Blake, naturally attract him. He borrows metaphysical devices from Giacometti and the vibrating color of his backgrounds from a number of abstractionists.

Having found his critical moment he makes it a semi-blurred ectoplasmic moment of becoming, which introduces the crucial dimension of time into his art, bringing one to his obvious interest in serial dissolves in film and the serial exposures of Eadweard Muybridge's studies of motion. The motion in Bacon's art is unique. He catches the spirit gawking out between moments of physical metamorphosis. The results can be spectacular. The center self-portrait in his "Study for Three Heads" is speeded up with multiple viewpoints and looks like a Picasso head of the thirties humanized by Hugo Van der Goes.

Bacon seems to have accepted the meaninglessness of life as a point of constructive departure, and despair accepted is as good a basis as any for making art. Tellingly he has referred to painting as a game, so one is free to replace the rules according to one's will. As a performer on this bridgehead he is a vastly compelling and compulsive artist—a sort of existential Expressionist, no moralist at all, and if he feels pity, it is overcome by curiosity.

The implication behind the perverse nobility, the despair canceled by acute sensation against bare nerve endings, is bleak. For life no treatment is possible, but we all have the cure at hand. In an inverted act of affirmation, his art is like a ceremonial suicide to prove the value of life.

October 1963
The New York Times

Miró's Violent Ceramics

So MUCH of Joan Miró's work has been a sort of delicate surgery on the unconscious—extracting its organs and forms with aseptic precision. In his new ceramics at Pierre Matisse's Gallery the surgery has turned into a kind of rape. Violence has erupted with an impact increased by the memory of Miró's previous discretion.

The effect is brilliant, uneven, definitely upsetting, further testament to the unease about his work Miró has had for years—he destroyed scores of paintings in 1959. This show may also be evidence that the precisely antic pictures that made him famous (and perhaps his own strict habits and immaculate person) were defenses against chaos.

Ceramics and sculpture are nothing new for Miró, who did some sculpture around 1922, began to think seriously about ceramics in 1942, and had his first show of ceramics in 1956. His collaborator has been Joseph Llorens Artigas, a master craftsman he has known for forty years. Working with fire has been deeply to Miró's liking, since it produces those chance accidents he finds so stimulating to creation.

Textures, rudely plowing into the eye, are a first and lasting impression because they are much more than usual surface entertainment. They express a deep sense of geological stress and of the process by which brute matter is ground and formed—a feeling confirmed by the dull lustre and earthy pungency of the glazes, and further confirmed by Miró's frequent admission that certain places and rocks and textures have always haunted him. The designs and incisions are made with a rough violence, animating the shapes of ceramics that might otherwise appear arbitrary. Indeed, some remain so.

Fired from the earth, the ceramics have a dominant theme also of the earth—woman as earth-mother. It is impossible to avoid the deeply sexual nature of these pieces: the apertures, the foldings, the foramena, especially in that bizarre and moving image of birth as a sort of geological phenomenon "Monument to Maternity." The same benign terror can be found almost anywhere in the show—a huge egg, with one wall folded into a great slit, is a smoothly violent expression of emotions easily recognized but less easily named.

It is this quality that makes the works profane icons devoted to instinctual mysteries. Miró also makes us realize again how much of modern art is rooted in Surrealism, and how underground and persistent its effects have been.

Miró's new ceramics are fascinating because they are in the direct line of his development, or perhaps because they overtly reveal formerly covert preoccupations. They are something that was necessary for him, and that almost frightening necessity manifests itself most of the time.

November 1963
The New York Times

Kurt Seligmann: Magic into Art

WHILE he still lives, even if he is totally inactive, a strange thread persists between an artist and his work. On his death the thread, a sort of metaphysical towing rope, snaps; the work is anchored in time and, finally separated from its creator, begins its struggle for existence.

How does Kurt Seligmann's work look now since he died in 1962 at the age of sixty-two? From the large show at the D'Arcy Galleries, he is still a sizable Surrealist whose highly individual pictures are mirrors of the universal Self. Looking at his art, it is still full of recognitions.

His images, raised by wheeling, flailing rhythms, ignore the pantries and cellars of the Freudian subconscious. Seligmann lifts one's eyes to a sky populated with tattered, unfleshed engines, pointing the way back to the cabala, to those magic compulsions the Irish call *geasa*, which make life a logical function of absurdities one is forced to accept.

Anyone looking at Seligmann's icy joustings quickly realizes that his ancestors don't have to be invented or tailored for him. With its maskings, costumes, improvisations within a persistent convention, his work is reminiscent of the Commedia dell' Arte, of those tattered seventeenth-century *memento mori* wood carvings and of such other Swiss as Fuseli, Urs Graf, and, as James Johnson Sweeney has pointed out, Niklaus Manuel Deutsch, who painted the "Dance of Death" in Berne. The dance, of course, is always there in Seligmann's work, sometimes compulsively elaborated into an icy delirium, sometimes (in the early paintings) restrained to the gentle trapeze work of Arp-like shapes.

The early work is classically Surrealist in the Arp-Miró tradition. The shapes float and wobble and swim alertly through space, as if it were some supporting fluid. Someone given Seligmann's work undated might arrange it in reverse, putting the late work, full of traditional associations, first, and ending up with the early Surrealism.

The exact relationship of magic—he wrote a book on it (*The History of Magic*) in 1948—to Seligmann's development is a puzzle. He felt it was "quite apart" from his art. But it seems to come in again and again by way of his concentration on magical substances, transmutation and metamorphosis. He thought his "magic philosophy" gave him a potentially unified view of all ideas, substances and experiences; and his art transposed everything into a world where they could act themselves out parallel to life, in a universal image of it. In the end there seems to be little doubt as to a magical basis for the beautiful diabolism of his animated vegetable world.

The paintings, of course, can stand up without it—proving their own existence rather than that of the doubtful ideas that make them possible. In this Seligmann reminds one of W. B. Yeats, that fellow cabalist, and there are a few lines from "Sailing to Byzantium" that are pure Seligmann: "An aged man is but a paltry thing/A tattered coat upon a stick, unless/Soul clap its hands and sing, and louder sing/For every tatter in its mortal dress." There is the same courtly passion, raggedly aristocratic, the same sense of gesture.

With Seligmann gesture is signaled by flutters of hollow drapery following the movement of absent limbs and body. When his figures are most recognizably human they are least successful—the distance between life and the imagination canceled. His figures need their alienation from common reality to make their comment on human identity, which leads to meditations on that identity as reflected in the mirrors and lenses and realizations the twentieth century puts around one.

Some of Seligmann's answers to that question are troubling—great shimmering trunks whose vegetable curiosity makes them wave around like decapitated Jack-in-the-boxes; creatures who, with tubes and proboscises like hypodermic needles, seem like elephantine enlargements of those animalcules clinging just under the surface of a pool. Sometimes they become too lurid in color, too close to science-fiction grotesquerie.

But the first and last point about Seligmann is that, unlike most Surrealists (who hold time still, who concentrate meaning by isolation) he urges his whole baroque world into a compulsive dance—a dance that is a stylized ballet of heraldic conflicts, terrors, joys, magical signs, that are, in the best work, elevated into the upper air, where they are eaten by excess of light. It is this conscious connection to the great conventions of the Baroque that puts such a gap between him and the exfoliative branch of Surrealism (i.e., Max Ernst's forests and geological jungles) that builds up emotion through clutter and excess. Seligmann was most truly a brilliant translator of ancient modes, symbols, and conventions into modern Surrealist dress. A brilliant and moving translator. But still a translator.

February 1964
The New York Times

Graham Sutherland

GRAHAM SUTHERLAND, who has proved that the phrase "English major painter" is not a contradiction in terms, looks like an intelligence officer in civvies. His face is brown and lean and gravely alert until two sprays of crow's feet fan out from his eyes as he smiles. His latest paintings at Rosenberg's produce a series of bright, blank shocks that withdraw to a disturbing distance as one tries to re-experience them.

For the outstanding thing about Sutherland's recent art is its compression of suggestions into snarled or flashing and darting forms which are pinned to an environment that tends to neutralize them. A psychological distance is established between the object and its presentation, an austere zone threatened by alien recognitions. This firm control of recognition allows a slight displacement of identity often far more disturbing than the usual Surrealist shower of multiple suggestions.

This displacement is the essence of metaphor, and his perceptions are habitually at its service as he walks the landscape in Kent where he lives.

"I often go for a walk in a big tract of land, half cut down, half forested. Suddenly I see something like a figure or an eagle sitting there—it can look like an insect or even a piece of machinery—and then you get up to it and see it isn't. This momentary flash, this glimpse of the thing, one gets for a very short time very often, but sometimes long enough to draw it. For I'm very longsighted, I can see detail in the distance. I've always liked to see things very near or very far. Often I draw things from long distance just for themselves, without recognition. Sometimes recognitions persist up close.

"I'm very dependent on actual things. I walk down a road—it doesn't make any difference the time of day—I see something exciting and extraordinary. There's a welling up of interest and a shiver down the spine." He smiled. "Like A. E. Housman"—whose physical symptoms of inspiration included eye watering and throat constriction as well as the shiver.

"This highly complex business of the initial inspiration is often a question of the purest accident—your mood, how you feel. By walking one is able to catch things unawares. One is very relaxed and one sees things even when one's not looking for them. The

35

leafy backgrounds of some of the new pictures simply arose out of one of those chance encounters. One evening I walked down the garden and saw them looking like that."

Typically he qualified the mystery of the encounter with a practical rider. "These chance encounters have to be tested first. They are often tremendously unrewarding. They have to be tested for your own personality, whether things can be done or not. This means drawings, experiments. The painting of the 'Head Against Leaves' was half finished before the leaves went in.

"What can be made artistic currency? In principle, everything can. But in practice, only certain things for oneself at a particular time. I don't think basically one can change at all. There is a certain essence in one's make-up that is—unfortunately, I think—constant throughout one's life, but there are different ways of finding that quality, thank goodness."

First he finds the image that compresses a landscape or figure back into its seed—"paraphrasing," he calls it—and then, like an entomologist, he mounts it in space and setting. "I don't know what color it's going to be or what environment the form is going to inhabit. The control of suggestion applies not only to form but also to color. I'd like things to be at once enormously involved psychologically and yet very detached."

This distance is what gives his new art the rigorous sparseness of archaic modes, while retaining their formalized expressive power. "I suppose—to be literary for a moment—it [his art] is concerned a bit with finding a vehicle in painting for what I see outside. To paraphrase, to rewrite in a different way, to make the actual thing more real, more potent by the rewriting. The poetic image? The only poet who has had an influence on me is Aeschylus. Extraordinary quality of metaphor—for instance, 'Dust is mud's thirsty sister'—a potent drawing of attention to the character of a thing by reference to another thing."

A case could be made for his art as a form of classic drama about the basic savageries that Greek drama deals with. For the displacement of easy recognition is like the masking of Greek characters. And the absolute frontality of his compositions is measured and formal no matter what enormity they contain. He speaks of Egyptian art, which still has a great influence on him, as "the supreme example of something psychologically tangible and yet very formal. That room at the Louvre, they are like real people and yet done with an enormous formality one hardly realizes.

"Do I want to get around the corners [of that frontality]? I would like to get around the corners. And I'd like to have a number of objects in the same picture."

Only another artist could fully realize the magnitude of these problems, so simply stated, problems whose solutions might enable him to realize ambitions to do "something as complex as Cézanne's great 'Bathers,' or Tintoretto's 'Worship of the Golden Calf.' "

May 1964
The New York Times

Henry Moore: Sculptor Between Two Reputations

HENRY MOORE, overdeified in the forties and fifties, is now paying the price. At sixty-six he stands behind two reputations that sometimes overlap. For many he is the man who revived an art dead in England for four hundred years, whose achievement makes him one of the greatest of twentieth-century sculptors. For some others he is a good, if overrated, sculptor, of importance in the thirties and forties, whose more recent work is inflated and portentous, retrospectively eroding his best achievement by revealing its defects. The exhibition that opened this week at Knoedler's shows how both attitudes can be read into it.

37

Perhaps this is because the values of the period in which he made his reputation are now archaic. Though they helped propel his work into prominence, they now—unless you still subscribe to them—detract from it.

In those days, a great deal was made of Moore's ability to transpose the body into geological equivalents—his metaphorical capacities. Metaphor in art is now a commonplace with a vocabulary of metaphors overused to the point of cliché. The Surrealist apologia for transposition and metaphor seems overcrude and simple now, too. Also dated is that form of idealism which perceives in weathered objects—stones, rocks, etc.—vast compressions of time and natural forces. And the attitude of "truth to the material" arising out of this now appears an odd morality, since sculptors have made careers by transgressing the demands of materials. These ideas seem a high-minded form of romantic idealism.

Such idealism doesn't wear well in art, since it tends, especially when threatened, toward "style" and rhetoric—those subtle corruptions of the creative impulse. Although these concepts were instrumental in rescuing sculpture from base forms of illustration and imitation, past necessity doesn't interest the present in the least. Moore's work now has to survive in a world in which even such attitudes as he expressed a few years ago seem dangerously impractical.

"It's only a great humanist," he has said, "a great artist like Giovanni Pisano or Masaccio or Rembrandt or Cézanne who can express the tremendous power of goodness that exists somewhere in human nature. Much as one admires Bernini, for instance, I don't believe that he creates wonderful human beings or leads to the idea that human life could be consistently marvelous."

So Moore is a humanist. And during his excursions into alien arts he has been in search of metaphors to express, by nonhumanist means, humanist ideas through humanist themes—the mother and child, the family, the reclining figure. His early and middle work show an obvious and engaging relation between these means and ends, which can be connected fairly directly with what he called his tough and tender sides.

But since the early fifties—just about the time ideas about art began to change drastically—the tender side seems to have got more of its own way. He flirted with a sort of romantic classicism after a trip to Greece in 1951. And some of his later sculpture has been almost Expressionist—bulbous and eroded in a way he may have learned back from younger sculptors who learned from him. His idealism, with a lifelong habit of metaphor behind it, attempts in the major later pieces to harden and solidify this romantic letting go in monumental transpositions. Which brings us to the big problem.

The later work—the totems, the divided reclining figures—is huge, its gigantism a form of mannerism forcing expression predominantly through size alone. The main metaphor is the body as a geological rock formation, thus emphasizing the obvious characteristics—durability, nobility, strength, etc. Now such rhetorical usage of metaphor seems unnecessary when the unaltered human form is becoming viable artistic coinage again. To some, Moore's use of metaphor seems like a man using strategies learned in a war that just isn't on any more.

Thus his reclining figures, particularly, can look, depending on your point of view, like parodies of the metaphor of man as geology. Their giganticism produces an inertness, a hyperstasis that is a parody of sculpture presence. This means of producing feeling while pretending to ignore it seems merely a high-minded disguise for sentimentality. By a curious failure, his metaphor becomes naturalistic rather than expressive—the leathery textures are more like cliff and rock than anything else, so the metaphor loses its power to illuminate the idea.

Yet, oddly, Moore's work manages to withstand the present laconic antirhetorical attitudes that cruelly expose his modes of thought and many of his sculptures' pretensions. The surrealist ideas of the thirties and forties, and those of the present—which produce the double image of Moore as Michelangelo and as has-been—seem curiously irrelevant to his work. What his late sculpture, with its self-consciousness, rhetoric, and exaggerations demands—in fact imposes—is a Mannerist standard. By that standard his work stands apart from the rage of ideas that distorts its value in either way.

June 1964
The New York Times

On the Death of Stuart Davis

STUART DAVIS was never what people nearly always thought he was. He was a loner, but he had a name for being a mixer. He looked like an indigenous All-American, but he was a man of great sophistication and charm—if you knew him. He had no time for fools.

His death removes one of the limited company of major painters America has produced. Although he had been in and out of hospitals, his death was unexpected. He was improving, he felt he had a new future, he had begun working again. Not being able to work had made him miserable. "I can't get the release that work gives you," he said when he was ill. But in the past year he had done some major painting. He was working on a picture the day before he died.

"Art isn't a commodity. It must mean something to the human race," he said not long ago. He tried to make it mean something every way he knew how. He was argumentative, a letter writer, a controversialist, a fighter. He saw sides and took them. He was downright, tough, and tender. He wrote a spare, balanced prose, tightly logical. He talked hip. His intellect was precise, his emotions numbered.

He was never out of date. Whatever happened in the world of art already seemed to have a precedent in his painting. His hard, dissonant color, his rigorous intellectual integrity, his use of words and letters in some abrupt aphasic alphabet of his own, all found confirmation in subsequent developments—as if the present had undertaken to prove his past.

His colors were snapping and staccato long before the new Optical art hit the galleries. And the word-obsessions that occur in Pop had a natural ancestor in him.

He was an urban animal. He united the febrile vitality of the city with an abstraction so firmly founded on principle that his art is classical in spirit, if not in narrow definition. Art and life collided and fused in his best work through the medium of a mind passionate for order.

The famous egg-beater series was an expression of that cool passion for order, for syntax, for discipline. He understood the vocabulary of form and color, and their creation of space, as few modern artists have.

When he talked about art, he talked with concentrated gnomic clarity, capable of shading meaning precisely. The violence and pungency of his work often depended on the most oblique and subtle shading of his means. This gave his art a firmness and durability that made it a standard of honesty on the artistic scene, a point of stable reference every new artist felt he had to consider in taking his own bearings.

A pioneer, he never profited greatly from the revolution he helped win—the cause of abstract art in America. He didn't believe greatly in revolution, he simply wanted recognition for the new ideas, not total triumph. "I'm in favor of ideas and their execution, but I don't think everyone has to be," he said.

He had no sympathy with artistic anarchy. "You don't add to tradition by destroying it," he said once. "I'm not interested in overthrow. I believe in permanent values. Isn't anything permanent for the future, in the future?"

This is the final paradox for those who saw him as some sort of hipster ancestor living at his nerve endings. The deceptively matter-of-fact exterior (he looked like someone who was going to go and shoot craps any minute) concealed a classic spirit, a spirit of the sort that could find some principle of eternal order in the neon wilderness of Times Square. He searched disorder for its unifying principle. Not long before his death, he told me: "The value of impermanence is to call attention to the permanent."

It becomes his epitaph.

June 1964
The New York Times

Edward Hopper

EDWARD HOPPER once wrote in a mock-serious letter that he might "try to prove [a] point by complete silence." His silence has always been formidable. Last week he broke it to summarize his art—replacing in one sentence the thousands of words written since his retrospective opened at the Whitney Museum. Each picture, he said, "is an instant in time, arrested—and acutely realized with the utmost intensity."

This week the 184 works were being crated for transport to the next showing—in Chicago. It really seemed as if what was being packed were freeze frames from a lifelong movie. For in Hopper's paintings the traffic of every day is stopped, the continuum interrupted and disrupted—the connections blown apart. The resulting isolation of impact imprints his images indelibly on the mind. With all his pictures booming around, it was difficult for even Hopper to take everything in: "Some pictures lost impact because they were hung with so many others. It was hard to concentrate." Each of

Hopper's paintings, like the moment just before crisis, demands full attention.

The subjects are completely unremarkable—an empty street, a semideserted restaurant, people lounging in an office. But what turns Hopper's isolated moments into majestic events is a vision which monumentalizes urban banality through means as geometric and solid as Cycladic masonry—given life by light moving across his pictures in oblique trajectories. Hopper's means are deceptively simple and he has spent a long lifetime—he is eighty-two—learning how to conceal them. Their effects now seem mysteriously without cause.

Rarely has a career been so strongly and singlemindedly sustained. Born in Nyack, New York, in 1882, he studied with Robert Henri, skirted the Ashcan School, Social Realism, American scene painting, and then, with an extraordinary display of stamina, simply outlasted them all. But he was a slow developer—thirty-one when he had a picture in the Armory show of 1913, thirty-three when he began the series of etchings that forecast his great paintings, forty-two when he had his first real success.

All the time he was observing with that implacable eye. He can hit off a stripper's muscular, lacquered sensuality, a woman's character in the way she shoots two fingers around a cigarette, or show passion gone stale in the back-to-back pose of two people on a bed. The sensuality is strong, but disciplined by a formal strength that is almost a moral force. Rarely, a playful impulse escapes—a flourish of horses' heads, clouds in a slow cumulus effervescence, painterly virtuosity in a glass ashtray shot through with light. Sometimes he breaks out in daring blurts of color (the red chimney in "Second Story Sunlight")—then conceals them.

The history of Hopper's art is obviously that of an incredibly acute observer—ever simplifying. It is the history of a clearing eye and a gathering tension. Its development lies in these eliminations, until simplicity is brought to the critical point where it pays the greatest dividends—a pocket history of much modern art. Color gradually becomes brighter and purer, the paint thinner and more translucent, compositions simpler but their equilibrium more complex. Every inessential has by now been burned away so that today he can approximate his deepest wish—to project the image in the mind's eye, without loss or "decay," as he calls it, directly onto the canvas—the artist's dream of absolute creative ease.

"It's nearly all thought out before he gets to the canvas," says his wife, Jo Hopper, a painter herself. "Once it's put down there's the minimum need for change. He just keeps strengthening the impact." As he worked at one picture, she saw "the intensity increase and increase day by day."

If any picture sums up this process it is his latest, "Sun in an Empty Room"—two pillars of light against the wall, utter vacancy intensely contemplated. Like all his art, it achieves impact through suspense, rolling over all the fragilities of doubt and chance and transience with a great assertive statement that is yet constantly assailed by them. After this it should be hard to paint another picture. But last week Hopper was "working around"—i.e., thinking about—his next work, slowly gestating the image he would project on yet another canvas with the "utmost intensity."

December 1964
Newsweek

Marcel Duchamp

"PEOPLE in the year 2000," said Marcel Duchamp, speaking to William Seitz of great modern artists, "will name the top five or six men." Duchamp, whose career has now been totally confirmed by recent history, is as good as elected—which doesn't interest him in the least. He has consistently sidestepped the calcification of

44

deification, methodically added to his myth by deflating it—has survived as a living mobile unit as no other great name of modern art has. "I believe in life being the expression of an individual," he said once. Life, not art, is the prime value.

But his art keeps asserting itself. A large sixty-year retrospective at Cordier & Ekstrom's Manhattan gallery opens this week. Assembled by Arne Ekstrom over eighteen months, it has already been bought in toto by a New York collector, Mrs. William Sissler, with the intention of presenting it to a museum—probably a college museum —as yet unchosen, a prospect to set every museum director into transports of discreet lust. How did the man who once said one's lifework could be packed in a valise (and who did just that) feel about having his whole oeuvre, his life's by-products, suspended over some anonymous American college. "I never expected this," said Duchamp. "It's a compliment. I don't mind."

"Not Seen and/or Less Seen," Duchamp's title for the show, passes up the great conventionalia already frozen in the Philadelphia Museum's Arensberg Collection ("Nude Descending," "The Bride Stripped Bare") to annotate many of Duchamp's less well-known encounters with life, for his works are the footnotes to a strategy of coping with life. "To be a painter for the sake of being a painter was never the ultimate aim of my life," he told Seitz. "That's why I tried to go into different forms of activity—purely optical things and kineticism—which had nothing to do with painting." But Duchamp's intuitive lunges outside the context of art are now art because the definition has been expanded to accommodate them. The age has grown up to them, is busily mining their ideas, programming their possibilities.

"Possibilities" is a key word. For Duchamp's art has been a one-man system of opening doors in seemingly blank walls, acts which still carry the nostalgia of departed shock mixed with rather Heraclitean forecasts and divinations of the present—and future. Going around his show is to see again the old ideas that, like Joyce's, simply won't get old: the readymades (the famous urinal, the snow shovel) selected à la carte from the dishevelment of reality and surrounded only with the magical aura of a new idea; optical arts shuddering colors and kinetic whirligigs; curious investigations of chance in controlled experiments, like the series of threads varnished where they dropped. Some of his old ideas are finding bizarre new confirmation—the robotization of love, the curiosity about sexual alignment (he created a fictional alter ego, Rrose Sélavy— from *C'est la vie*); the disposability of art, with its limited life span—after which the "emanation" goes, what's left being suitable for museum interment; and above all, the idea of art being secondary to life, important only as a way of staying alive in the interstices of organized society's shrinking mesh.

He is a unique human animal, the classic model for the strategies of coping. There is still, at seventy-six, an obliqueness about his frankness. No matter how directly he looks at one full-face, one's basic composite image of him remains unchanged—the blur in which the lean Jesuitical face, the occasional flutter of bony hands, the dun-colored presence, the confessional-soft voice, add up to a pat asceticism—and yet, of course, he is not ascetic at all. The confusions that have surrounded Duchamp arise mainly from the simple fact that he does not share the common unconscious assumptions by which people think and act. His life is an enigma to others but not to him. "Doubt," he said once, "is everything." He has carried this through to a doubt in conscious existence, which, carried further, eliminates death itself.

Like nearly all the great creators of the twentieth century, he has lived his life in an acute awareness of what produces that doubt— absurdity—and has developed a high tolerance for contradictions, often using them to cut off the spoor for those following up fast with logical intelligence. Duchamp has managed to experience fully and beat the time he lives in with acts of paradox, evasion, summation, assumption, and metaphysical wit. The performance cannot be lost by calling its by-products art and studying *them*. For Duchamp, in the ultimate and logical paradox of his progress, is the anti-hero as genuine hero, who projects a vision of man that is surprisingly heroic in the Romain Rolland tradition: ". . . a man . . . an individual; a demigod who, if he is not crushed by the opposition he will have, will come out of it and conquer a position above the complete leveling by the great mass of the public. We don't know," he adds, "what qualities he must have. . . ."

January 1965
for *Newsweek*

2. OUTSIDE THE MAINSTREAM

Patrick Collins, Dubliner

IN 1950 Patrick Collins painted a picture which he called "Stephen Hero." With a Georgian house as backdrop, lit by a single gas lamp, the skinny figure of Stephen Daedalus, elegantly awkward, makes a wandlike gesture with a stick. Behind him, through a window, a woman is visible. To the left, a carriage disappears up the telescoped perspective of a street. Predominantly brown and umber, the whole scene has a drifting subaqueous character, like a distillation of Dublin atmosphere on certain evenings. It is a key picture for the understanding of his difficult art.

Collins had in mind that moment from the nighttown scene in Joyce's "Ulysses" when Stephen says ". . . so that gesture, not music, not odours, would be a universal language, the gift of tongues rendering visible not the lay sense but the first entelechy, the structural rhythm." It is typical that so abstract a statement should have preoccupied him. His own attempts to achieve communication are, in their way, as personal and hardly won as Joyce's.

He expresses feeling and awarenesses that are impossible to put into words: a certain atmospheric awareness which, through memory and myth, is associated with his own childhood and with his own country. He feels his country deeply, its loneliness, its eeriness, its constant motion through changing light. With long twilights, the Irish air fosters ambiguities and uncertainties; at times objects, and indeed, the events of real life, seem to lose their reality or to take on another reality. It is this quality that has been described as permeating the Irishman's view of reality; its philosopher is perhaps Berkeley, and it amounts to a distrust of the senses. In Collins' work there is a constant and ambiguous shift between what is seen and what is known, what is present and what is absent, what is felt and what is remembered. His art is perilous and strange, the product of a rare imagination.

Patrick Collins was born in Dromore West in County Sligo in 1911 and grew up in the same county as the Yeats brothers. As with them, it has haunted his imagination; one of his finest paintings, his latest major work, summarizes and celebrates the landscape of his youth. His formal training was limited to a couple of evening terms at the National College of Art in Dublin; for a short time after he worked in George Collie's life class and in a few other studios. A flatly realistic self-portrait from about this time shows a young man slumped in a chair, staring at the spectator with a glance that is direct and yet veiled. The whole attitude of the figure is introspective, and Collins, a big man, appears shrunken and withdrawn, and rather puzzled.

Apart from occasional visits to the Continent, he has lived and worked exclusively in Dublin, first in a studio in Parliament Street, and more recently in Dermod O'Brien's old studio in Pembroke Lane. He works slowly, carefully bringing each picture to its full realization. His work has been seen in England and America—most recently at the show of contemporary Irish art at the New School. He has had two one-man shows at the Ritchie Hendriks Gallery in Dublin. In 1958 he received the first prize in the Irish section of the Guggenheim International Award. Curiously enough, this was for a picture called "Liffey Quaysides," full again of Joycean associations.

Collins' early work moved steadily to a style that seems to have grown directly out of his own experiment and meditation. It is difficult to point to influences; he has always been aware of his isolation. He has certainly been influenced in attitude by the remains of an art he describes as "always unfinished and fragmented, always under the ground": early Celtic and early Christian Irish art. Later, following this source, he went to Brittany to experience more closely the spirit of the great tumuli builders.

His earlier canvases were usually predominantly of one tone or color, gray as if misted, or brownly aqueous as if steeped in peat water. This gave one a sense of space which extended beyond the frame, and made one rather harshly aware of its limitation. Texturally his work was of great richness, in its glazing and reworking with a dry brush recalling, more than anyone else, Santomaso.

This textual circumference within which the action and points of focus occur is curiously the first rather than last part of his art, like a substance that must first be laid down or secreted by the imagination. Within it, that imagination, having created its own ambience, can function. This texture had its greatest richness in the early fifties. It consists of a web of strokes, crossing and recrossing, and done over again with an almost dry brush to deposit little edges of paint, brown or eggshell blue or yellowish-green, which trail and hang across the canvas like torn edges of silk. Collins is almost obsessive in obtaining this texture and feels compelled to work and rework until finally satisfied.

At first sight one sees only this breaking, subtle texture with its tiny clots of paint. But gradually it dissolves and the eye is left wandering inside a tinted mist. Slowly one discovers presences slid into the space, creating planes and movement. In many pictures these shapes require long acquaintance before they identify themselves, partly due to a tendency to multiple viewpoints within each picture, and to an ambiguity in depth which moves the objects back and forth in planes. Sometimes the object dissolves in atmosphere, at other times passages of paint run together to call the object more definitely to mind. Here is a balance between recognition and nonrecognition which moves attention back and forth from the object as object to its abstract function in the total picture. In an early work, "Dublin Apple Seller," the figure appears, conjured up from among the surrounding shapes, then constantly relapses back to become a meaningful and disturbing entity of its own. It resists the attempt of the observer to classify, identify, and comprehend. In "Sea Castle, Howth," the building floats like a cloud between sand and sky; at other times it takes on, through rectangles overlaid in layers like shelves, the solidity of cubic forms. His work exploits the psychological fact of perceptual ambiguity—when an object switches indefinitely from one recognition to another and back again. This is not a technical trick but is deeply felt and implicit in his view of life.

The effect of all this is to leave one with a sense of something half grasped, half understood, half realized. And this flirting with the eye, annoying it, stimulating it, tricking and frustrating it, and then carrying it on again, is a little like a similar result, produced by vastly different means, in the labyrinths of early Irish manuscripts. In a way, too, it is these qualities that make his art a suitable (unsentimental) instrument for the Celtic myths that some of his titles recall: "Aengus of the Birds," "Children in a Legend."

His view of the Irish countryside is influenced by an awareness of its immense age. He is the only painter I know who can capture the nuances of feeling which the Irish countryside provokes, especially at dusk when it is haunted by innumerable memories. In a picture called "Landscape with a Round Tower" the landscape like a crumpled tablecloth is seen from above. The impression is that the moving eye has focused on something and then moved on. Always very aware of the way in which the frame shears off and limits, Collins here makes one aware of extension outward, so that the picture gives a feeling that beyond the physical limits of the frame the scene trails off somewhere into mist, loneliness, cold.

His landscape, then, is altered by memory. It exists as a mental coordinate of the landscape seen at twilight in certain parts of Ireland. Certain stretches of marshland and rock have intense nostalgic associations, as if the country's history had gone into the soil and left its people with a sense of unfulfilled youth. It is a rootlessness that becomes an ache. Patrick Collins' pictures extract this quality, and recreate visually the mythic aspect, the troubled absence. They remain in the memory like a length of film holding remembered but undeveloped images. He has mentioned, in contrast to all this, how his first sight of an English village struck him like a blow, a stated fact. It was so unambiguously *there*, so real and certain of itself, that it safely canceled mystery.

This is a tremendous amount to get into any picture. It is Collin's achievement that he has evolved an original style that allows all this to be expressed. There is a complete consonance between what is expressed and how it is expressed, between his subtle, formal and elusive associative elements, that is the distinguishing mark of the genuine style. Since it is a style dealing with impalpables, with the ghosts of ghosts, it fares badly in group exhibitions. When Collins is asked to talk about this style, he has difficulty and is reduced to attempts at description of the experiences his pictures project.

The strength and endurance necessary to create an individual—and contemporary—style in a country without a modern tradition in art he has gained from a complete confidence in the sources both within himself and in his environment. "I know that what I want to paint is *there*," he says. He explores in a darkness charged with poetic potential. In that darkness his pictures have their slow gestation—which for the onlooker is re-experienced in the difficulties of extracting their theme and essence.

In this search, his integrity is notable. "Despair is an ingredient of every picture." Once he finds himself on the track, he trusts completely to instinct. "It's like being given a gift—something given; afterwards you don't know where you got it . . . afterwards you wonder at it." Each picture is an exploration in a place where nobody, not even he, has been before. As his work matures further, he seems to gain more confidence in his gift; some of the later paintings are superb in their confidence and strangeness. The confidence comes from a belief that his pictures exist somewhere in his mind before he starts painting them; as he says himself "I have only to find them." He feels himself guided in a labyrinth of choice until finally the pictures discover him.

His art, then, is one of instincts and intuitions. It exemplifies that strange Irish distrust of the senses, which on occasion seems to open areas of delusion and illusion—the dream of a world which does not replace sense experience but is almost a particular variety of sense experience. The aspect of things which is preserved I can only call "presences"—the strangeness of things without sign or symbol, without that naming of objects and phenomena which enables the adult to function in a world of miracles. This quality is, in essence, in his statement: "It is the aura of an object which interests me more than the object. I see a few bottles on a table and I feel there is something more than a few bottles. It is this something more that I try to paint." Perception and memory here unite in this quality of focus, a concentration and intensification of the emanations of things that are a property of their presence. Collins, in his way, belongs in the category of the uncategorizable—Samuel Palmer, Odilon Redon, Morris Graves (who likes Collins' work). He is, in fact, in his singleminded search to make the impalpable palpable, a sort of mystic, a hard-drinking, humorous, profane kind of mystic, as many tough Irishmen, suspended between heaven and hell, are.

Patrick Collins is by any standards an important painter, undoubtedly the most important living Irish painter. His art is born out of his environment to an extent unusual in modern art, and it finds poetic symbols for the Irish tragedies—absence, unfulfillment, the anguish of nostalgia. In his way, he adds, as did Jack B. Yeats, to the iconography of his country by giving substance to an impalpable dimension in the elusive Irish mind.

Spring 1961
Studies

Hyman Bloom

HYMAN BLOOM once said with a serious air, "There must be lots of people I haven't met." There are lots of people who haven't met Hyman Bloom. He pursues his craft in seclusion and with an almost monastic dedication. He is something of a legend in Boston, and what Hyman Bloom is painting now is hidden behind the deceptively fragile but iron curtain of his silence. Creation is a private affair.

When, four flights up, you knock at the door of his Dartmouth Street studio, the voice says, "Wait a minute"; inside, a canvas is taken down and turned to the wall, the door slides open, and brown eyes contemplate one from a serious and secret face. Then in an extraordinary transformation, the whole face changes with welcome. Thus Hyman Bloom introduces you to two Hyman Blooms, and there may be others that I have not yet met.

The two Hyman Blooms share a face of extraordinary mobility. Its most stable expression is one of rapt and brown-eyed seriousness, with the glance reflectively sidelong, as if he were slightly distracted in listening to you by the duty of keeping a third interior eye on his own thoughts. From long practice he does this so well that he achieves the impossible. He is the only person I know who can be warmly remote. But produce a thought that fascinates him, and his face breaks into all kinds of fluid and responsive attention, and expressions chase each other across his face like whippets of wind across a pond.

Walking with Hyman always gives me a feeling of potential, as if something extraordinary were going to happen in a prosaic Boston street. He walks as if the next buoyant step were going to lift him. I always have the impression that some day, with no surprise at all, I will see him walk up step by step from the street beside me, on some invisible staircase of air.

He was, of course, marked from the start, when Harold Zimmer-mann, a Boston artist with strong theories about teaching, found two young geniuses (Jack Levine was the other) in Boston's rough South End. Zimmermann was a teacher of almost military disci-pline, and he insisted on an exacting training of drawing from memory after intense observation. It is discipline that marks Bloom to this day. So much so that the presence of a model before him can still induce a sort of paralysis. For him the gap between observation and creation is a highly gestatory interval during which a great deal of hidden machinery is silently turning over.

I once asked him to do a tiny picture, with one condition. I would supply the model—a dried-up old apple of which I am very fond. Then the fun started. Hyman delights in this sort of ridicu-lous dialectic.

"If I'm to paint an apple" he said, "you must allow me the freedom to paint it as I wish."

"Full freedom. All I want is the apple."

"Do you want it alone or with something else?"

"I don't mind. That's up to you."

"I don't know if I can really express myself in an apple."

"Well, you like Caravaggio's moth-eaten apple."

"What sort of an apple would you like? A cubist apple maybe? Or a futurist apple?"

"Just my apple. Only you must paint it from life."

"From life?" said Hyman, with mock apprehension. "Do you want to destroy me?"

This is not as funny as it sounds, however, for Hyman's inner eye surrounds any artistic problem with a number of intensely vivid images, which his capacity to visualize calls up with almost eidetic force. His very fertility of invention and the possibilities he con-fronts diminish his output.

Zimmermann's influence was complete for about six years, until Hyman was nineteen. Then he and Levine were taken up by one of Boston's great pundits in the fine arts, the late Denman Ross, who

55

had been long associated with the Fogg Museum, an institution perhaps justified in taking itself so seriously. When Hyman met Ross, he was Professor Emeritus at Harvard, a man who behaved grandly in the great tradition of patronage. He hired a studio where Zimmermann could instruct the two boys, and after their graduation from high school gave them each an allowance of $12 a week. Ross also gave them the benefits of a theory of color he had developed through which precise effects could be repeatedly achieved by a strict limitation of means. Thus color could be manipulated like the notes of a musical scale, and complex effects produced by simple combinations. He also introduced them to Oriental art and to the old masters and their drawings, which the two youngsters studied avidly. They developed a formidable respect for tradition.

Bloom's early drawings under Zimmermann are young master drawings, and, like the glass flowers at the Peabody Museum, they are among the major Boston phenomena. They are incredible achievements for a young boy, with a resilient sureness of line and a facility that is breathtaking. Often of metamorphoses fixed in transition, they are metaphysical weddings between fact and fancy performed by an introverted and almost painfully sensitive imagination. They remind you of that middle air where many of William Blake's apocalyptic figures suspend themselves. I remember one drawing of a bull or animal with human head, like the beast in Yeats' poem, shambling toward Bethlehem to be born.

It was around 1943 that Bloom paid that strange, historic visit to the autopsy room at Kenmore Hospital and contemplated the human fragments so pitifully exposed. As he looked at them, the silent marriage between painter and subject took place in the imagination, and out of this mysterious moment some of his greatest pictures were born, many of them years later. In that one confrontation he studied the sheen of fascia and tissues, watched the rapid color changes in exposed viscera, and stocked that avid memory of his with all their subtle changes against the exposed field of red. Many years later he was to return to the autopsy room, this time at the City Hospital, to satisfy an anatomical curiosity. He remembers that the doctors were often surprised at autopsy when they discovered the cause of death.

He has searched then, with surgical devotion among the chasms and abysses of viscera, like some mystical materialist, for a physical coordinate of pain, or for some ultimate metaphysical abstract, like meaning. Although meaning, like knowledge, is something, he finds, that continually recedes with greater understanding. But it is a rich journey.

Like Baudelaire, Bloom is fascinated by the erotic beauty of decaying flesh and the sensuality of attraction in repulsion. He delights in finding a subject that makes a sort of plexus through which such contraries can move in and out, like breath, and restore the spirit to what has become inanimate. I always consider Bloom a religious man, and for many years his cathedral was roofed by the Gothic vault of the rib cage that covers man's most intimate vitals. His act of creation has often taken place among maimed and exposed and glistening entrails.

He doesn't talk about art—mainly because it has little to do with art. It would be like him to say that no one tries to explain John Donne in terms of painting. Nor does he think a painter should be under any obligation to talk about art. His enthusiasms are for music rather than words. And outside his door you are liable to pause to hear the single note of an Indian flute being put through a progression of adventures. Carefully and with much love he takes from special cases sitars and ouds and vinas, stringed and bulbous, and he draws from them the wayward rhythms and subtle dissonances of Indian music, his head bent toward the instrument as if he and it were having a conversation. He is willing to talk about music endlessly. I remember one memorable sight of such a conversation—Bloom and the composer Hovhanis in conversation in a Greek restaurant. Hovhanis, lank and prickly and bearded, inclined across the table toward the shaven Bloom—a satyr in earnest converse with a Jesuit.

Once we got lost in a museum and Hyman said, "Why are museums so big?"

"Because fellows like you keep painting."

"If it were only me," said Hyman, "it would be a very small museum." He paints very slowly. And part of the mystery of Hyman Bloom is the disparity between the huge total of hours he spends behind the closed door of his studio and what comes out in the way of painting. He denies that his creative parturition is excessively painful. He has no difficulty in finding a subject, and he has chosen a definite repertory of subjects—chandeliers, corpses, buried treasure, brides, mediums, séances—because he feels that these are subjects that can reflect his total preoccupations with life and art. The only problems are the painter's problems, finding the shapes and colors which trap the vagrant spirit.

His studio is a large, low-ceilinged room inhabited by an extraordinary collection of objects. A skull without a mandible still manages to smile from a shelf; not far away is a photographer's 8-by-10 camera on a tripod. In a corner behind it a dried fish's head hangs from a string, the naked skeleton trailing out of it like a bony feather; there is a row of tools hanging up; an elaborate recording machine in another corner; a photograph of a Bronzino young man; beside it, Bresdin's print of the Good Samaritan. There are dried-out leaves and flowers, still and brittle with decay, that would shatter at a touch. Scattered here and there in the studio are other paraphernalia and incunabula of his vision—fossils, shells glowing with tiny concentric rainbows. All that glistens takes his eye.

Hyman was seven and one-half when he came to this country from Latvia, a place so fertile of American painters that Russia, if it has a mind to, can claim to have invented a great deal of contemporary American painting. His earliest memories of Latvia are vivid and shocking. This was during and immediately after the First World War, and to the young boy the facts of war had little to do with the ideas behind it. There were, he remembers, Germans and two types of Russians, and what he saw left him with a violent antipathy to all ideas of progress by physical violence. The human animal is an instrument of profound evil and profound good, and the mystery is impenetrable. Morally he is a realist, and partly stoic.

Through the wry façade of irony and the thorny thickets of wit one can see some large convictions resting uncompromisingly, like boulders. He expects nothing from the world and, expecting nothing, owes it nothing. He has nothing to do with schools or fashions or popular causes. He is suspicious of the doubtful blessings of professional success, and the paternosters of directors and dealers. He has the creative artist's respectful contempt of the scholar, and the creative artist's mistrust of the critic—with Hyman, an indulgent mistrust; I think one could find in him a belief that paintings are, for critics, modified Rorschach tests in which the critic always discovers himself, and may stumble across the painter by accident. He also extends his contempt to those artists whose favorite topic is the insensitivity of the patron and purchasing fund to their work. The expectation of success is to him a vulgarity. One is not ultimately judged by one's contemporaries, and one's contemporaries don't matter very much. His perspectives are awesomely wide, and it is this that makes him seem like some astronomer watching his thoughts circulate like planets. It is this that absorbs all bitterness and leaves only a wry irony.

He seems to find his affimation where facts are reduced to echoes. When with him, the safe world may suddenly lose its bottom and leave you treading air. He riddles every seemingly solid fact out of existence, and leaves it suspended among a wilderness of mirrors. He surrounds the fact with so many points of view that our eyes are distracted from the fact to the many ways Hyman sees the fact. A great deal of Hyman's life has been dedicated to the conquest of many points of view around the same fact. To test an invented point of view and make it solid and accessible to others through his art is to him a major achievement. Perhaps the slow struggles of his painting are an attempt to make the unsubstantial world solid again, and to synthesize life's fragments as he wishes, into the coherent and wordless language of painting.

Fall 1961
Art in America

Torres-Garcia: The Journey of an Unusual Mind

JOAQUIN TORRES-GARCIA was an Uruguayan who wandered all over the Western world and died at an advanced age in 1949. His personality and ideas attracted a coterie that—especially since his death—has canonized him.

Now and then his work appears and receives mixed reviews, many of them expressing frank puzzlement, and his exact position in the history of art is liable to show fluctuations until his reputation finds its level. His followers claim for him a position among the giants of the twentieth century.

A selection of his works from 1928 to 1945 is on view at Royal St. Marks. It illustrates the journey of an unusual mind into unusual avenues of communication.

Communication indeed is the key word to Torres-Garcia's life and art. A man of large humanity, he apparently dreamed of a universal alphabet of symbols, gleaned from the records of the ancient and modern world, that would be legible to all humanity. Through these symbols his personal experience could be expanded to transfer the communal struggles of the race.

His messages are painted with a grayish-umber palette and lit by slanting light so that they look like aged, incised stones and tablets. The symbols, many of them anachronistically from the modern world, are reminiscent of Egyptian hieroglyphics crossed with Pre-

Columbian ideographs. They appear like the glyptic meditations of some private and wayward mysticism or, more fancifully, like the records of our own civilization awaiting excavation and interpretation after our extinction by some future catastrophe.

Each picture is a compendium of symbols, numbers of which are gathered into boxes of varying sizes. In one box are a house, a fish, a branch, a dove, a snail, a cow—presumably symbols of pastoral peace and plenty. Other boxes in the same picture are more complex and mysterious—one contains a heart, a scale, a helmet, a hammer—and the total significance of these is anybody's guess. One may speculate, if one likes such games, about the conflicts of impulse (heart?) and reason (scale?) and the solutions violence (helmet, hammer?) often forces on such conflicts.

Other recurring motifs are an anchor, the top exaggerated to a cross; biological and algebraic symbols, often like some queer arithmetic of the imagination; a clock persistently stopped at ten to eight (or twenty to ten?). Like many who try to communicate directly through universal symbols, he ends up with enigmatic notations to a system of ideas.

Since the pictures can only be deciphered with the aid of written ideas, the paintings illustrate the ideas but do not illuminate them. Like a form of artistic cybernetics, they code "bits" of information to transfer a theory that constantly tends to desert them and leave them without meaning. For the initiated they are eloquent. For the uninitiated they remain mute and dumb.

Their muteness is not disturbing, and this is most unfortunate. For they lack the sheer artistic meaningfulness and gnawing urgency that will not allow us to rest until we have come to some understanding. You can take them or leave them alone.

Thus, solving Torres-Garcia's symbols is an intellectual game, not an artistic experience. And although there is a certain degree of pleasure in noting his references to ancient ideographs and languages, these references do not, of course, prove he was a great artist, they only prove he was educated.

Torres-Garcia was a universal humanist and a maker of symbols that will be sources of endless delight and perplexity to information theorists. He was obviously a great personality and a man of sincerity, learning, and imagination. All this is, however, irrelevant to his capacity as an artist, and that capacity, while at times brilliant, is far from major.

He must remain among the lesser phenomena of this half-century, a minor James Joyce among artists whose messages remain mutely inverted. I think his exact position can be found by placing him alongside Paul Klee, a man who succeeded where Torres-Garcia failed.

Klee was first and last a great artist. Torres-Garcia was not. Klee's symbols were born in the darkness of the human heart and illuminated with a rare intelligence.

Torres-Garcia tried to graft his symbols with admirable tenacity and ingenuity onto the universal human heart, but always from the outside. He was a greater man than artist.

January 1962
The New York Times

Philip Evergood

PHILIP EVERGOOD, a leading figure in art, can currently be seen at two galleries, ACA and Dintenfass. Whatever else his paintings prove, they prove emphatically that Evergood is an uncompromising individualist. Thus, people tend to like or dislike his art. They are rarely indifferent.

Evergood's themes in these two shows move between social realism and allegory. His social side is often noisy and rambunctious, at times wide-eyed and innocent. His allegories have gusto, imagi-

nation, and some surprising symbols: an angel blowing a hot
trumpet, a large fat bird about fourteen feet tall smugly watching a
convention of skeletons.

One excellent picture called "Grandstand Play" (1946) shows
some assorted animals having a recklessly bibulous time while a
horde of admirals watches an atomic-style cataclysm that sinks a
navy, flicks an observation balloon out of the sky, and blows the lid
off a capitol dome. It is full of good painting and profitable suggestions. More recently Evergood has begun to paint lyrical portraits in
broad, loosely applied pastel colors. His range is wide, his sympathies large, his point of view definite.

In nearly everything he paints there is a certain forced awkward-
ness. This is the element that his admirers admire and his critics
criticize. At times, both are right. This awkward, semiprimitive and
fetchingly clumsy elegance can be effective as fuel for his imagination when it is taking off for the upper air of symbols and
allegories. It can be an irritating mannerism (mammalian hands,
wide eyes, knowingly simple postures, etc.) when he stops to admire
it himself.

This quality, however, is in his imagination; it is not externally
imposed. It is not in itself destructive, for it is merely evidence of a
dramatic sense. It can be an asset or a weakness, depending on how
it is handled. Unfortunately it has a tendency to become egocen-
tricity of an indirect kind, which draws attention to itself only to
say, "I'm not really important at all. I only happen to be at the
center of the stage."

Evergood does not need to descend so regularly to this sort of
secure insecurity. To make art out of oneself is fine, but it must be
done cleverly, not cutely.

However, Evergood has met all the challenges of twentieth-
century life head-on. Motorcars, bicycles, perambulators run in and
out of his pictures; he has taken on jazz bands, slums, dance halls.
Race prejudice, mass murder, war, atom bombs and cruelty bother
him, and he has done something about them. His appetite to take

in the world and to give nearly everything a visionary aspect seems to be associated with this headstrong quirk in his imagination—this egocentric naïveté that tends to become mannered sophistication. His twists and turns in the worldly labyrinth to avoid the destruction of this naïveté give his figures a tortuous air, and even put curlicues in his signature.

He is a critic's headache. You can say he needs more self-criticism. But more self-criticism would destroy him. His virtues are the cause of his vices, and vice versa. It's often very irritating, but that's the way it is, for better or worse. Thus he is often very good and often very bad, but nearly always interesting to watch.

May 1962
The New York Times

Andrew Wyeth

Andrew Wyeth, that painstaking microscopist of the familiar, is having a large exhibition of drybrush and pencil drawings at the Morgan Library. They show how he carefully carries a precarious insight along with him to encage it in the finished picture. It is a practice that emphasizes his isolation in this age of the spontaneous, the improvised, the accidental.

For Wyeth is anathema to the inheritors of the mainstream of modern art—the tradition based on color as form and on abstraction as an event. Conversely, he is loved by the antimacassar school of Victorian academism. The former fate will not disturb him; the latter may.

However, it's doubtful if anything disturbs Wyeth, far from the battlefields of aesthetic warfare. We have had plenty of examples from the battlefield of the Artist as Insider, the Artist as Outsider, the Artist as Anarchist, and the Artist as Academic Revolutionary.

Wyeth is a refreshing example of a great American tradition: the Artist as Loner. He flourishes in isolation, contemplating his own equivalents to Walden Pond.

Isolation is the key word. Wyeth's artistic position is isolated, he isolates himself at Chadds Ford outside Philadelphia, and his work is often a study of desertion. Even the people he paints adhere to some strategy of avoidance—they look a little wooden, they turn away from us, sometimes they sleep.

There is more psychological penetration in the signs of human absence—a pair of old shoes betrays the most intimate identity of its possessor; a detached hand, treated like a still life, becomes a window to the personality; a used coat is a mute witness to the past. From clothing, that most intimate of environments, he expands his interest to other immediate surroundings: houses, and outside the houses the familiar landscape, long lived in and studied.

From these familiars, Wyeth slowly distills a poetry of association and remembrance. Thus his art, for all its acute observation of wind and weather, is highly literary. Again and again the nostalgia of past experience is quickened by rediscovery in his book of nature. His world seems rooted in a lost childhood, and he searches with physical persistence in his foregrounds, like a gardener with a magnifying glass. Though his close-ups have a tradition as far back as Dürer, they remind one as much of certain passages in Tennyson and Wordsworth.

Constantly close to a literary theme, his art is in constant danger. On occasion, the poetic associations remain attached to the drawing instead of being recreated through it. And the elusive insight can evaporate in bearing it through the drawings to the finished picture, which then becomes descriptive prose instead of lyric poetry. Also he has a distressing tendency toward the picturesque, as betrayed by the horribly cute Landseer eye of the "Hound." His great ability is to organize detail so that it fits perfectly into the whole, like the mechanism of an exquisitely worked watch.

Most of his parentage lies in nineteenth-century America, in the themes of Winslow Homer and in the detailed exactitude of the American primitives. Indeed, he has many primitive traits himself, notably his unsureness of space—where an arm doesn't go up the sleeve, or where a crouching boy is stuck onto his background like a cut-out. And his light, one of his main actors, is reminiscent of the solid luminist light of nineteenth-century America. It does not define the solidity of forms, but quietly irradiates a mood. It pours up from under near and far horizons like a reversed waterfall, turning the world into a vast stage.

In one other way Wyeth is pure American—in his total respect for the fact. The existence of the fact makes it inviolable. A model is not just a model. It is a familiar such as Tom Clark. The bedspread on which he lies is not just any bedspread. It is the one made by Tom Clark's grandmother, and Wyeth respects its existence even when the crazy-quilt colors prove difficult to handle.

Thus his pictures are a living encyclopedia in which the facts are preserved, a dictionary of feeling, annotated with love. The record of his contact with life, these facts become the touchstones of a private mythology he openly makes public. As Agnes Mongan points out, "Inanimate objects—an abandoned oar, an empty crab-shell, an abandoned house—are vivid with a symbolism no less valid for its simplicity."

Wyeth has a last lesson. Since history demands trends, movements and chains of events for its comprehension, we confuse historical value with aesthetic value. Wyeth is far from the mainstream. He demonstrates that the ultimate importance of an artist's work is not in the extent of his influence or the revolutions he provokes. It is in the artist's work itself—in the degree to which his world, no matter how far away, can take possession of us. Wyeth's does.

April 1963
The New York Times

Coney Island Rubens: Reginald Marsh

DIVES DEFY RUM RAIDS, blared the headline in the New York *Evening Graphic* sometime in 1930. FINNS FIRE ACROSS SOVIET BORDER—MOLOTOV PROTESTS PROVOCATION, said the *Daily Worker* in November 1939. Between these two dates came the repeal of Prohibition, La Guardia, Jean Harlow, Dillinger, the Lindy—and the best of Reginald Marsh, two of whose paintings in his retrospective at the Gallery of Modern Art contain these headlines. They also contain the seamy asphalt jungle through which Marsh sends his sweet-faced, large-thighed floozies walking innocently as cows.

A lot has happened since Marsh, a post-Ashcan man in theory and practice, was last seen at the Whitney Museum in 1955, a year after his death at fifty-six. World War II eclipsed him and his generation, except for a few tough survivors. American regionalism gave way to internationalism. Abstraction overwhelmed the exhausted high-mindedness of social realism. Now, in this cool, new-minted age, when sign language is the artistic mode and rhetoric is considered emotional prostitution, how does Marsh look? The answer is a big surprise. Marsh looks good.

His huge and voracious appetite for reality now seems more modern than Ashcan. "Go out into the street, stare at the people," he wrote in 1944. "Go into the subway. Stare at the people. Stare, stare, keep on staring." His sense of temporal crisis makes him sound like an Abstract Expressionist: "The head always filled with ideas for pictures is hindered in their execution, or rather, the execution is energetic and impulsive but the result disorderly and inadequate." He was obsessed by motion and action. His clusters of nudes building up to horizonless compositions writhe like Abstract Expressionist paintings in which the brushstrokes are whole figures. Of Coney Island beach, a favorite subject, he wrote, "Crowds of people, in all directions, in all positions, without clothing, moving—

67

like the great compositions of Michelangelo and Rubens." Here is the clue to his success and defects. He bodily hauled the grand manner out of the past to do over modern lowlife. His picture making was always conventional, but his subject matter often wasn't.

How an artist sees himself is as vital as what he sees. Marsh's Hogarthian self-image plugged into the big power outlet of Rubens had elements of self-deception that explain a number of things—his programmatic lack of introspection, his human types that remain too typical, the lack of insight below the skin. It explains too, as the juice gave out toward the end, why all that was left was the posturings, the empty faces, the feeling alienated from the form to produce those Mannerist old master drawings that critics in love with safety admire. The alienation was partly because his subject had betrayed him, the city had turned from Minsky's to war and his self-image couldn't make the switch.

But in the thirties his storytelling rhetoric, his shouting Whitmania ("How good it is to be alive and able to paint, not all of every day but for all of most days, yes!") projected a true image of the city in one vital way—its speed. For all its fleshy opulence, Marsh's New York is the ruthless time machine where tomorrow's newspaper is already obsolete before midnight, where the tense is always future, and life can only be snatched at through the continually flawed moment of the present. Marsh identified himself and this crude juggernaut with the American dream—his art is a joyful Yes to the colossus rushing forward, throwing off the human debris. In the great days, he was swinging with the city, with the billowy strippers whose curves threaten to fly right off, the rows of burlesque jerks in their faded plush, the fallen bums still vital with the city's baroque energy. The acid of satire never bit—his vision was all energy and delight.

Critics will find it easy to dismiss Marsh's work as cruelly dated—the figures stilled in poses that self-consciously proclaim their pedigree, the city embalmed by the hopeful application of old-master formulas. But now, after we have been bombarded by the cinematic face half a block high and made self-conscious about a matchbox, what rescues Marsh's pictures from their thirties time capsule is mostly the artist's connoisseurship of American oversell, the majestic pitchmanship of PIP AND FLIP, TWINS FROM PERU; NO TURNS PERMITTED; DANGEROUS CURVES; ELECTRIC TATTOOING DOWNSTAIRS. Now all this has the legitimacy of life held at the self-conscious distance of art. But when Marsh—joyful vulgarian of the Grand Style—used it, he broke a sign-blind convention: you didn't paint the words, or at most, you blurred them.

Perhaps it was because Marsh was a former cartoonist and newspaperman, two roles conceivably married in his art. The cartooning of the Grand Style represented his ambitions. And the headlines, the posters, broke through to him in the newsman's passion for the word. The two roles were deeply connected. He could only embrace the public image while shielding himself from its banality with the great traditions.

December 1964
Newsweek

Jack B. Yeats

A CIRCUS TENT collapses like the mad flap of a solitary wing. Plucked by currents and cross-currents of air, an island vibrates in the distance. Within a room, walls ripen into shadow, the light teems on a face, a rose, a hand, in a dazzle of fickle energy. In all the forty-five pictures at MIT's Hayden Gallery, moist Irish light teases out into half-spectrums, flickers over figures and landscapes, imparting a sort of bucolic aristocracy to the mundane.

The vision is unique and it belonged to Jack B. Yeats, who, shortly before he died at eighty-six in 1957, said, "There is nothing more for me to paint." What he painted was nothing less than the swan song of the outsider—in a country where all were outsiders, the British Empire's white Negroes. He celebrated and triumphantly concluded one of the world's most attractive legends, the Irishman as romantic. In him, the heroic age of gods and heroes was fused with the everyday event, until a commonplace was thrust up into poetry by one of the most powerful racial memories in the world.

There were plenty of gods and heroes in Jack Yeats's lifetime, living and dying in revolution, giving birth to the "terrible beauty" his older brother, W. B. Yeats, wrote about. Wrote Jack Yeats: "The true painter must be part of the land and of the life he paints." Jack Yeats was. At nineteen he witnessed the tragedy of Parnell, later lived through revolution, civil war, and the growth of a new Ireland. His work is the single great correlate in visual art to the literary heroic age of his brother, to Joyce, O'Casey, and his friend J. M. Synge.

It was a miracle that it happened at all. The rest of Irish art was bogged down in provincial imitation of English academism or in tentative experiments with one eye cocked on Paris. Yeats did the obvious—and difficult. He unself-consciously painted the life of the people, a collection of individuals no one had been able to put together into a nation, in the tradition they understood—that of the outsider. The swaggering tinkers, acrobats, and sailors shouting, singing, storytelling, fighting their way through his work are the true inheritors of the nomadic Celt, suspicious of cities, always in favor of the escape route that keeps the spirit active and alive. He adapted the same method—in his paintings and in his picaresque plays and novels that cross Tristram Shandy with some of the methods of the arch-intelligence of Irish letters, James Joyce. For Yeats the escape route was always open. "An artist," he wrote, "should avoid convention, even if the conventions are his own invention." It is the same temperamental strategy others of his race applied brilliantly to the devious labyrinths of political intrigue, talk, and poetry—the hopeful trinity of the dispossessed.

Jack B. Yeats

To an Irishman, Yeats's work is full of the baffling complexities that summarize an Irishman's narrow plot of earth. Jack Yeats assuaged a country shrunken with bitterness through the healing gift of poetry, which was not new, and through the gift of elegance, which was. "He gets Watteau-er and Watteau-er," wrote Samuel Beckett to Tom McGreevy, and this exhibition is full of the ragged elegance of tinkers and actors. In "Tir nan Og" the boats and figures arrive at the (literally) Land of the Young. It is another Cythera, wilder, coarser, the figures moving with an instinctive natural grace, a grace country people sometimes have.

His art continually brings one back to wonder. He exposes the infinite possibility present in the simple meeting of two people, he plums the mysteries and loneliness of departures. You can see some of this in "The Parting of the Three Ways," where the figures separate before a changing Irish sky, rippling with light as if it were alive. In "Free or Slave," he returns, as he often did, to the elemental moment of individual conflict in which one must die, reminding one that Yeats—and Ireland—had lived through civil war.

Outside Ireland Yeats is mostly just a name, the poet's brother, the unknown master who refused to let his paintings be reproduced believing each a unique event ("The better they are," he said about reproductions, "the worse they are"). He is misunderstood as an Impressionist, an Expressionist, a poetic genius in a cabbage patch. What he really is is the painter of his country's heroic past, the "thrill and tramp of memories," the travail of its modern genesis, the fluctuating temperament of its pre-Mass Man people. Painting the Irishman as hero in heroic times, he became the twentieth-century impossible, a great national painter whose work expresses a vision of the national character—a character which, in the new Ireland bustling with factories and foreign trade, is already invested with the nostalgia of departing myth.

February 1965
Newsweek

3. THE LAST AVANT-GARDE

Robert Motherwell

ROBERT MOTHERWELL's work is fascinating for a number of reasons. He has long been one of the leading names in the avant-garde and a consistent practitioner of uncompromising abstraction. His talent is a curious and unusual combination of intelligence, introspection, and distilled emotion, all coming carefully together to create accidents on purpose. Rarely however, are these components melted in the heat of the creative act.

For Motherwell creates in what might be called an objectively introspective fashion. The objectivity places a chilling distance between the observer and the creative act as viewed in the finished painting. Maybe this is a virtue. But it leaves Motherwell in danger of relentlessly proving private theorems to his own satisfaction and of performing too distant experiments in creativity. Thus the spectator tends to be ignored, which is not a virtue or vice in itself. It becomes one when the performance is hermetic, as Motherwell's tends to be.

In this Motherwell reminds me of another highly intelligent practitioner of another art, the poet William Empson, especially in his later poems. There is the same bloodlessness, the same intelligence, the same attempt to concentrate the essence of a medium—in Motherwell's case, of painting; in Empson's, of language.

In fact, A. Alvarez, in an essay on Empson, could be describing Motherwell when he speaks of work that is "cool in tone, wry, controlled, and unimpressed"—if we leave out the "wry." Both are highly sophisticated and tend to perform with themselves as audience, not because of an excess of subjectivity, but, paradoxically, because of an excess of objectivity. Both lack heat.

In two recent suites of small pictures titled "Caprice" and "Beside the Sea," Motherwell avoids intellectual decoration. A few bands of cool color throw up a spatter of paint that is held in midair as if caught by a high-speed camera. This lyrical Abstract Expressionist comic-strip sequence is fascinating in its demonstration of artistic curiosity, though in a rather sparing and arid way. The exact chance moment has rarely been so isolated and examined in painting.

Motherwell also continues his series "Elegy to the Spanish Republic" of which there are three examples at Janis' in his latest show. In them the artist flexes his muscles and beats the stretched canvas like a drum with huge blots and dashes to make some silent thunder. Closer inspection shows that he maintains the same cold distance from the act of creation, and the variations, though highly inventive, tend to fade into highly intelligent manipulation. (At least one of this series, "No XXXIV," is, however, a great painting, the great painting that Motherwell is always threatening to paint.)

These works invite two judgments. They are too simple, with their main interest concentrated on the double-take provoked by the quick evaporation of interest. Or they are too complex, the result of esoteric researches in which content is intellectually rather than creatively formulated. In a word, they are too easy or too difficult, and Motherwell does not remove his pictures from the horns of this dilemma.

Again, something from the same essay on Empson applies here: ". . . generalizations are clarified, but they are not intensified. They are transformed almost into abstractions, ideas to be proved, commented on, illustrated, but no longer to be felt out."

Motherwell, in my opinion, has always tended to illustrate rather than to imaginatively transform ideas. This emphasis has tended to misdirect his art from what is to me his real virtue—a genuine lyric gift that could be expressed harmoniously and unpretentiously by fastidious abstract means—which is, tellingly, a description of some of his best collages, where the small size of the work seems to have released him from the responsibility of being "major" and impressive.

December 1962
The New York Times

Herbert Ferber

HERBERT FERBER, whose retrospective opens at the Whitney today, is a leading member of the New York school. He is regarded as a pioneer in vitalizing an enclosed space, most notably a room at the Whitney Museum in 1961. At fifty-seven, Ferber can look back on a life unsparingly devoted to sculpture. His development has been steady, although opinions will differ about the results.

Obviously a man of talent, Ferber was one of the advance guard of American sculpture in the 1940s, submitting himself to a variety of influences that modified a native vitality. His work at this time metamorphosed the human figure into a number of styles, and his instinct for space, the sculpture's sine qua non, seemed sure and searching.

In the late forties his work became thorny and predatory, contrasting bulbous buds with toothlike serrations, and growing organically into space like an inverted shrub. There were a number of parallels with Surrealist painting. At this stage Ferber was a talented and forceful sculptor, his abstractions heavily tainted with symbol and myth. Since then Ferber has changed drastically, and his course seems intellectually rather than naturally determined.

"Game II," a brilliant little lyric done in 1950, signals a change toward the decorative and the abstract. In the fifties, large vertical sculptures mimic plants with embarrassing closeness. "The Sun, the Moon and the Stars II" and "Running Water" are decorative translations rather than creative images, with a random and wayward formal logic. Ferber's sculptural instinct seems to have abandoned him, his sculpture blurred by attempts to particularize or generalize too widely.

After this, Ferber's sculptures prod outer space despairingly or are anxiously crabbed inside a delineated space. In his marriage of different forms, his handling of space, his balance between space and solid, Ferber broke all the rules. This is the tragedy of his sculpture. Its daring is undoubted. But so, in general, is its failure. The main reason for that failure is a failure of instinct. In a curious way, Ferber seems blind to the organic development of form in his careful concentration on the space it displays.

There are moments in the fifties when Ferber remains fascinating for the parallels he provides between sculpture and painting. "Cage II" in 1954 is an attempt to create three-dimensional calligraphy varying thicker elements with wires that curve and tangle. It is like a sculptural translation of Jackson Pollock's space, which was created through similar wiry dynamics.

In the sixties Ferber has concentrated heavily on pushing his churning calligraphs through a cramped space in an attempt to animate it. These calligraphs depend on a small vocabulary of curve and spiral and are extraordinarily arbitrary, lacking either psychological or formal justification. There is a sense of clumsy agony, all the more troublesome since it is unintended.

Occasionally, as in "Calligraph, Three-part," 1957, one can see what Ferber is getting at—sculpture whose vitality is initiated purely by its forms, whose energy is consummated by their marriage, whose enclosed space is animated in every atom of air. Unfortunately his work rarely provides such an insight. His later spatial adventures leave one with the sense of a talent pushed by an honest and uncompromising sincerity beyond its limits.

Yet, almost two years after this review was written, one came across one of Ferber's sculptures—at the Whitney Museum annual of 1964–65—which fulfilled exactly the criteria his work suggested but failed to measure up to. Called "Homage to Piranesi," it was notable for the way in which it pushed, with an almost physical shunt, large and ugly calligraphs through a box of space defined by his usual bars. Here, in at least one work, was the triumph of will over talent, the fruit of a relentless pursuit of inventive excellence from a base that seemed to preclude it.

April 1963
The New York Times

Hans Hofmann: A Style of Old Age

HANS HOFMANN, whose work of the past decade was recently put on view at the Museum of Modern Art, has finally converted me—something of much more interest to me than to Mr. Hofmann, who, showered with honors, is the Grand Old Man of avant-garde American painting.

He is a very young Grand Old Man. Anyone who has watched the blunt radiant face and stubby fingers animate an idea will find it hard to believe that Mr. Hofmann hobnobbed with Matisse, Delaunay, Picasso and Braque in those pre-Cubist years of modern art's stone age. His best work has only made its appearance in the last decade, a fact which, since he is eighty-three, is phenomenal. So is the main quality of his work—a joyous, weight-lifting vitality.

One must conclude that he is one of those rare ones blessed in old age.

A style of old age is usually marked by its uncommon fusion of profundity and facility, the reward of a lifetime spent at the battle-front. "It comes more spontaneously now. In the early days I had to go through more struggle for realization," he said the other day, sitting in the midst of his new exhibition, the pictures exploding all around in the shattering blues and reds of a great colorist and a born painter.

As a born painter it is in his genes to paint marvelously—the moment it leaves his hand the paint is alive and kicking. He has the warmest, coarsest, most opulent color sense of any modern painter. Along with intelligence and a lust to cover canvas, all this adds up to talent of a magisterial order. Yet outside the last decade there have been few masterpieces.

For there is a vital difference between the exercise of great gifts and actual creation. In Mr. Hofmann's work one had got used to settling for the evidence (of his gifts) instead of the event (the painting that would make his gifts incidental to it). His paintings could never quite tear away into self-sufficiency—there was always that penultimate sense of something unfinished, open, unfocused.

Perhaps this had something to do with his deeply thought out ideas of what painting should be. Basically, they deal with the fundamental ambiguity in modern painting—between the picture surface and the illusion of depth created within it through color alone. Through color are created forms, energies, recessions and relationships that in turn create a pictorial space, which is constantly forced to return to the surface to acknowledge the picture's two-dimensionality. This is the arena (first charted by Cézanne) into which moods and energies are projected, indivisibly fused with the means of expressing them. Here spontaneity and improvisation are vital—"you cannot preconceive a work." Painting thus becomes an immediate, urgent, almost physical encounter.

Mr. Hofmann's theories, not unnaturally, provide some clues to his past performance. He has, in my opinion, tended to rely over-much on color to produce form, something that accounts for the insecurity of his earlier work. In his rigorous refusal to avoid any preconception of what the painting should be, he tended to take too much dictation from the canvas, slipping into a sort of painterly activity that quickly escaped into frenzy or elegance. The great success of the present exhibition is that it has a stability and a focus that have allowed Mr. Hofmann's superb talents to finish some superb paintings.

While there are a few works of dashing ferocity and a few light lyrics feathered sparsely onto white canvas, the real meat of the show is the blocky, rugged paintings—to me his main contribution and a major one. They vary from splendid meditations on nature (tranquility recollected in violence) to some almost classic works of great solidity and power.

The latter are those in which Dionysian energies are anchored by radiant rectangles of pure color, his "pillars of light," as Mr. Hofmann calls them. These blocks of color or space sometimes occupy the entire canvas, building up like Cycladic masonry, im-mensely weighty or immensely airy. This marriage of the geometric with unconfined energies breaks the rules of good form, and in breaking them and getting away with it, extends them. The union of the dynamic and the static, the Dionysian and the Apollonian, is always highly precarious.

The squares are "Cézanne brought further," says Mr. Hofmann. For Cézanne color is volume; for Mr. Hofmann volume becomes energy. Perhaps that is why they stay together. The energy, dynamic in the flow of paint, is held static in the rectangles. It is an energy that warps the canvas, projecting ambiguous space, hurtling like lava, vibrating in rectangular lakes.

It is a remarkable achievement. Outlasting most of the Abstract Expressionists he helped to father, Mr. Hofmann has succeeded in holding that movement's violence within a rugged, semiclassical discipline, and has in a way done to it what Cézanne did to Impressionism. As well as ending an historic era he helped begin, Mr. Hofmann, in these paintings, offers a new point of departure.

September 1963
The New York Times

Adolph Gottlieb: The Dualism of an Inner Life

ADOLPH GOTTLIEB painted "The Frozen Sounds, Number I" in 1951. Reading from left to right, it shows a blunt dash, a red globe, a blue-black globe, a flattened red rectangle, and half a squat oval, all in a cotton-puff sky. Underneath is a level horizon holding down what looks like a scabrous, angry earth. It was, in retrospect (a twelve-year retrospect is provided by the current Marlborough Gallery show), a decisive point in his art. After that he went from strength to strength.

This show, excellently selected and introduced by Martin Friedman of the Walker Art Center in Minneapolis, is the one that brought Gottlieb the Grand Prize at the São Paulo Bienal last fall. It provides a convenient point to look at the career of an artist who was a fringe member of the Abstract Expressionist complex in the late forties and who has come decisively into his own since the group dispersed.

His development is thus a parable of the coming of age of art in America (from provincialism to sophistication in one hard abstract lesson) and also a parable of the artist's progress. For Gottlieb around sixty is infinitely better than Gottlieb around forty, when he was doing those surrealist pictographs that marked his escape route from realism. From Gottlieb and others, a case could be made for art as a middle-aged man's job, the artist coming into his prime, like a surgeon or a lawyer, in his fifties. Modern art is full of ruined early talents and late developers. Gottlieb is one of the latter.

"The Frozen Sounds" solved the main problem for an artist of his generation—discovering or inventing the motif that is both a declaration of individuality and viable for development over a long period. Anything more than one motif was considered a dispersion of the self, a confusion of self-identification. This rigorous limitation raised a number of problems—the most important being how to force simplicity to that critical point where it can imply maximum complexity, and keep it there. He solved it slowly and painfully. Once he solved it, he became brilliant.

Since 1951, his art has mostly annotated an inner life in terms of two elements composing a single motif—a globe above, the tangled earth, or a spatter of calligraphy, below. Together these elements compose a simple union and opposition that can express almost any duality you can think of—any duality whose union depends on conflict or balance: male and female, action and inaction, thought and feeling, ego and id, Yin and Yang. As Mr. Friedman puts it in the catalogue, this interplay is "in essence an expression of the paradox of civilized man who attempts to find equilibrium for those opposing tendencies which are a necessary part of his internal and external life."

Thus the criterion of Gottlieb's art is the extent to which his projected inner life remains vital—how he and his pictures (they become the same thing) stay alive. One watches closely to see if the permutations his units go through—the lateral shifts, the pulls, tensions, vibrations—retain a hold on one's feeling.

To some extent this is every artist's problem, but Gottlieb, by stripping it down, forces himself to confront it more nakedly than most. He has his failures, through oversimplification, through occasional dead space; but by and large he does magnificently. His motif has orbited into electrifying new fields of color, the horizon dropping away completely, the globes, usually single, now taking on a new radiance, raised with an almost palpable transgression of gravity as they dip and swim steadfastly over the explosive calligraphs below—writhing, kinking, hooking, contracting, precisely exploding —all the verbs are active in this extraordinary visual grammar.

Perhaps they retain this life because Gottlieb is an empiricist who proceeds picture by picture. He has never formalized a theory, never pushed his forms into overt symbols of a system. His forms inhabit a very individual area. One expects them to be more intellectually abstract or more psychologically forceful. They are neither icons nor ideal diagrams, but nonrhetorical materializations of an individual's moods and phases. Gottlieb is a very fine artist, growing still, an old-guard individualist who could teach the younger collectivists a lot of tricks.

February 1964
The New York Times

Gorky: Private Language, Universal Theme

FROM the barest facts of his life Arshile Gorky would seem, like Van Gogh, to be a natural for popular canonization. A life full of *angst*, self-dramatization, disappointment, terminated at forty-four, in 1948, by a melodramatic suicide, is ready-made romantic myth. But his art won't collaborate. It resists assimilation, distortion and dilution because of one formidable obstacle. Gorky evolved a new language, and its difficulties are a protection from popular corruption—which is ironic in itself, for his themes are as universal as the means of expressing them are private.

His fifty drawings at the Jewish Museum show that language in formation and in action, transposing common reality into symbols referring back to that reality in a shower of suggestions and allusions that turn a fact into a constellation of ambiguities. A fact thus becomes a process. It is an elliptical, demanding process, a bit like

81

listening to a familiar language and yet recognizing only every third word.

As language it is expression through two modern methods that have become traditional—displacement and ambiguity—the second a natural consequence of the first. In a period when realism had in general shown itself a blunt instrument in handling complexities of thought and feeling, displacement into ambiguous symbols was a necessary form of alienation, of establishing distance. One has only to look at some of his earlier paintings—the 1937 self-portrait in the Museum of Modern Art's great retrospective in 1963, where the arm becomes a sort of dumbbell that would answer for any limb—to see the deep-seated necessity to transpose things symbolically as a method of dealing with experience impossible to handle with explicit associations (*i.e.*, realism).

Thus Gorky is most truly a poet whose symbols pulse with the associations he forces to converge on them. Such concentrated symbolic thinking is more a poet's method than an artist's, and in looking at Gorky's work one often thinks of poets and the usages of language—of a sort of abstract surrealism that you might get by crossing Wallace Stevens with Dylan Thomas—fastidious intelligence excavating the visceral with a deliberate impatience.

The impatience is always there—early on when he went through influences like a man leafing through a book on modern art, and later when he turned each picture into a sort of narration continued in the next. It becomes a kind of extra process that identifies itself with his unstable symbols of growth, development, and change. And it constantly gives his art a sense of crisis beyond the delectation he occasionally allowed himself—a sense of art as personal crisis that he passed on to the Abstract Expressionists. Constantly probing at the limits of expression, he analyzed and synthesized until the two processes began to mimic each other, and motifs turn up so often that, like a biologist, one can recognize their morphology, partial origin, and hybridization.

The motifs are derived directly from the embryology shared by all forms of life. Embryology is incidentally the study of possibilities constantly being rejected by normalcy as it develops. Gorky's knuckles, membranes, and clefts realize these possibilities by elegantly circumscribing animal and vegetable processes with the same steady, implacable line.

Gorky's achievement does not take on its true perspective until one realizes the quality of his synthesis and survival—for he is a successful conclusion to a type of American artist with a high mortality rate, the immigrant arriving with a culture more or less imprinted on his brain cells (Gorky was sixteen when he got here from Armenia), coping with America and the problems of art as imported from Europe, trying to make a synthesis both as man and artist. Fortunately, when he couldn't go to Paris because of the war, the war delivered André Breton and the Surrealists to him.

It is at this stage that his final paradox emerges. As he perfected his language (the word suits his art better than "style") he began to look more like a transposed old master in disguise—his drawings defined a motif, were frequently squared off for translation to canvas, where a process of further improvisation took over, leading to different versions of the same painting, as if ambiguity of content had to be realized in a number of pictures. And old masters, especially Uccello, were regrown according to his embryology.

But the more he looked like an old master in disguise, the more modern he became. For the re-experiencing of a motif was vital to the art that came after him, as was his transference of a genuine improvisation to a large canvas. So was his precise automatism with its miraculous sense of process and the present, as well as his later masterful counterpoint of line and color as separate things composing a flat filamentous space. If he seems very much of a modern old master belonging to the first half of the century, he was also a source of the new by his very perfection of that end—an unparalleled triumph of eclecticism.

May 1964
The New York Times

Richard Diebenkorn

RICHARD DIEBENKORN is one of those sensitive tough guys who does it *his* way; an All-American who quarterbacks his career with greatest brilliance when the odds are against him. In fact, the image of Diebenkorn as quarterback gives some good mileage before it breaks down: tall, rangy, still youthful at forty-two, he looks like a quarterback, he thinks out complex moves and powers them through with a great arm. He succeeds big—and fails big. And in his private ball game he takes a lot of punishment, is sometimes buried by onrushing difficulties. He has to be hurting to know it's good—another American in search of the ethics of adversity. His retrospective at the Washington Gallery of Modern Art demonstrates that he belongs in the big leagues—the main line of American modernism from Hopper to de Kooning.

What does Diebenkorn play his big game with? The trivia of seaside suburbia—a woman sipping coffee, a disheveled tabletop, figures sunstruck in California's endless light. But though the scale is large, and the technique steamrolls paint around, the obvious is stated with such subtlety that the eye is battered, yet seduced. He has created works both monumental and casual, a rhetoric without rhetoric, the triumph of style masquerading as nonstyle. It wasn't always that way.

For Diebenkorn was once the hottest of abstract hotshots on the West Coast, a brilliant stylist who at thirty-three switched to realism. Ever since, there have been two Diebenkorns for most people (even his collectors are divided, backing one Diebenkorn against the other). In all the fuss, few noticed that Diebenkorn was being consistent—in his wish to change, to escape from his listing in modern art's Yellow Pages, his desire to grow and feel the pain. But on the sidelines everyone was taking sides, using him to fight out the battle of Realism versus Abstraction—a quarrel as dated as arguing the merits of Deanna Durbin.

Instead of a split personality, what Diebenkorn exhibits is clear evidence of integration. The early abstractions are filled with dark shapes of stabilized power, shot through with occasional lightning derived from Clyfford Still, the eminence grise of American painting. In succeeding years, Diebenkorn absorbed de Kooning and Gorky, and their idea of process, change, activity detonates his abstract paintscape.

Gradually the hovering abstract world feels the strain of gravity. Earth is pulled down. A lip of sky shows at the top. The space at center buckles under a big triangular thrust, and his failures in this metamorphosis—muddy, incoherent, and slightly desperate—are records of suffering rather than paintings. Then the figures, mute and stock-still, materialize in this abstract limbo. "I came to mistrust my desire to explode the picture and supercharge it in some way," says Diebenkorn. "I think what is more important is a feeling of strength in reserve—tension beneath calm." Now he is coping with problems he was bound to run into sooner or later. For when his figures recover from their concussion, he—and they—come up against the whole figure-painting tradition of European art.

So the tension he speaks of is the arbiter of Diebenkorn's success —or failure. In this judiciously selected show (by Gerald Nordland) the failures have been pruned out. Only a few remain as evidence of what happens when the big play doesn't come off—a few filleted nudes sag in puffy curves, the paint collides but the impact is muffled. Yet Diebenkorn refuses to cosmetize his failures. Only the big men have that sort of courage. The failures were unpruned in his last show at the Poindexter Gallery in 1963. There one could see how subject, technique, and the abstract impulse quarreled frequently enough to cause trouble. One nude existed in angry failure between abstraction and representation, a few housescapes won their struggle for prettiness, some heads built up of colliding ledges of paint could not cover their basic banality with mere impact.

Elsewhere he stepped out of the contest for his own tension-ridden solution to confect a delectable trifle, a moment of pure self-indulgence in a small still life—like a postage stamp stuck on a love letter to the past of Manet and Bonnard.

The five major pieces in that show—big pictures, of which two turn up in the retrospective, were—and are—solidly impressive. They look as if they were done by some muscular, big-thinking Bonnard or Vuillard with a coarse appetite for the extensions of Californian space—extensions as identifiable indoors (in a large sink) as out. One outdoor vista is pure Diebenkorn—a rim of houses seen abruptly over a window ledge, which they rush forward to meet with a definite slap, telescoping two planes into one, that the eye constantly tries to drag apart again.

It is in his handling of this kind of space that Diebenkorn, a real pioneer, has it over the other members of the so-called California new-figure painters: Park, the first to try to make figures exist in a post-abstract-expressionist space, the romantic Bischoff, and those intelligent schoolmen Wonner and Petersen—who, by the way, sometimes look much better than Diebenkorn, as followers are apt to do to the casual eye. Diebenkorn's pictures show the signs of trouble, sweat, failure, and success.

He forces his space to exist with an almost austere implacability— by twisting forms a little askew, through perspective hints, through the rush and advance of color that gives his work such an aggressive impact. As long as his abstract sense dominates, pulling the figure around with a no-nonsense anti-humanism that leaves it isolated and forlorn, his work will keep on the right side of the line dividing something new from something old in modern dress. When the subject forces its psychological demands, his work loses that "tension beneath calm," and becomes a tame addition to the European tradition.

It's a tough spot to be in. Relax and you've lost it. Keep it up and the figure can only survive in a sort of paralytic crisis—from which some may want to draw morals of the modern predicament. Predictably, then, Diebenkorn is turning to landscape and still life, avoiding the figure (one splendid tabletop picture, slightly reminiscent of a Francis Bacon in its construction and sinister greenbaize color, has only a hand as a sign of human presence). He may test easy solutions but he doesn't stay with them. Like the best American painters, he has that moral itch that pushes him back into the painful struggle to keep crisis at bay.

He is a major artist partly because he is trying to keep the impossible possible through a blunt attacking strategy that seems a very American solution to the problems of past and present, subject and abstraction, technique and know-how—and what to do with them. He remains one of the best and most genuinely thoughtful painters around—with future indefinite.

November 1964
Newsweek

Willem de Kooning: Grand Style

As HE WALKS AWAY one sees a smallish man with radiant hair, a loose, striped jacket flopping over black corduroy pants—and the rear view has some of the pathos of Harpo Marx. Then he turns to present the shockingly perfect classic head and the direct blue gaze in which wisdom is a sort of mobile innocence. If he never painted a picture he would be extraordinary—for one is always aware of the fluctuations of his identity, the ebb and flow of tensions and possibilities.

But he has painted—and his pictures have opened up a new territory other artists have colonized. Some have fenced off small plots in de Kooning's majestic acreage. Others have moved off from it to new country of their own. His impact on the scene has been

87

enormous, his financial success complete. For most people, his achievement and reputation make him *the* American painter.

He exists very much in the present moment, between the pull of the contradictions he feels fanning out from every decision. The tension of their drag keeps him teetering—almost dancing—with a high nervosity, as if life consisted in some act of balance, like walking a high wire—or in an image he himself provides, riding a bicycle, as he pedals the roads around the Springs, near East Hampton on Long Island. He has lived there since 1961, not in his new house, which is still building, but around it in other artists' places: Wilfred Zogbaum's, John Ferren's, and now Nick Carone's.

The contradictions come up in everything, and he has an anti-attitude to resolving them that is in itself an attitude. "Someone asked me to sign for the release of Siqueiros"—the Mexican artist once accused of trying to kill Trotsky, later jailed for "social dissolution," and now released. "I didn't. But I wouldn't sign against him either. I didn't have the details. It's like Trotsky. To one he's a hero. To another he's an assassin." The wish to keep the whole field of experience shifting manifests itself in everyday things. He won't pin down the future by making an appointment, refuses to allow the modern oracle, the telephone, to interrupt his day.

His constant electrification by the make and break of contrary possibilities should result in fatigue and impasse—and it sometimes does. It is a risky way of life—with art a part of it—that keeps the motion speeded up so that a new perspective of dilemmas constantly replaces the old, telescoping behind him a history of strategies, solutions, innovations, surprises. The movement keeps him in crisis, confidence constantly assailed, innocence constantly renewed.

This life style is reflected in de Kooning's work, as it was in the other painters of his generation, such as Jackson Pollock and Franz Kline. Their problem was how to *live* a picture rather than merely to paint it safely, how to take *action* (Harold Rosenberg called Abstract Expressionism *action painting*) when all the powerful solutions of art history pluck at every stroke. Unprotected by the past, each stroke becomes a positive action among dangerous alternatives. Like any man of action, de Kooning is fond of sport, especially boxing. ("Are you a painter?" said Gene Tunney. "Yes," said de Kooning, humbly.) As in sport, there is a network of programmed possibilities within which high skill can make the chance hops and bounces work for it. Talking or painting, de Kooning adjusts to the possibilities like an athlete, shifting his balance, jerking his head around, lunging like a fencer to make or explain a stroke.

From the city to East Hampton de Kooning has transported a monad of the Abstract Expressionist ethos—himself, his model, his pad. And the pad is the apotheosis of the loft generation's dream. "It's really like a large loft," he says, "the best studio you'd find if you were looking for it. It's *found*." The roof kinks down to meet the upthrust of metal Y-beams, walls are suddenly interrupted by glassy space, the internal structure is full of catwalks and balconies, beams hurtle abruptly down, elegance is often forced into awkward corners. The huge rectangle of the studio is tilted into a rhomboid, a memory imprint from his old studio on Tenth Street, because "you can get the light better."

"I haven't any illusions about being an architect," says de Kooning, "but I always wanted to build a house." Bets have been placed that he will never finish it. For the loft-mansion, as expensive and lavish as the most ornate example of East Hampton style, turned out to be subject to the crises of testing, just like a de Kooning painting. "If you don't like a painting," says de Kooning, "you can wipe it out. This overhang—over the front door—took five days to build. Now it has to go." The house—first a sketch by de Kooning, then a plan drawn up by the architect Oscar Niemeyer, then a building subject to constant modifications—changes over the months like a huge 3-D painting in slow motion. Already it contains a history of additions, subtractions, and erasures—like a painting. De Kooning's inability to decide a work is finished, to separate himself from it, is one of the art scene's prime myths—so there has been total fascination with the idea of de Kooning painting inside a de Kooning house, inside a mobile metaphor of his own dilemmas.

Now he is painting again, on a door (he recently bought six to paint on) standing in a slot on the studio floor into which it can be lowered "so you can get to the right spot without a ladder." What is on the door has changed and changed—but the basic image has ridden the current of change like a bather: a levitated pink jelly-baby, the impastos like frayed silk, her eyes bobbling foolishly in the rococo Elysium he is trying to get into. Last year he sketched her ancestors, dozens of them, two by two in balletic free fall, "very cozy together," he says, "not very avant-garde for me." And then he adds—the king annoucing his abdication—"I don't want to be new any more," which in a contradictory backlash is a new attitude indeed.

Always he has failed to step into the blueprint for his future. So, going backward through his art is as surprising as watching it unfold from the beginning. "Art never seems to make me peaceful or pure," he said once, "I always seem to be wrapped in the melodrama of vulgarity." Going backward one encounters the hurtling pastel pinks and blues of his abstract landscapes, his Revlon period (late fifties), the ferocious "Women" wearing the banal All-American smile (early fifties), and in 1948, the year he burst on the scene at the Egan Gallery, those electric paintings of white lines swerving and rebounding in the darkness as if tracing the courses of charged particles.

To go back beyond 1948 is to follow him into the underground, where his talents made him a marked man before the public ever heard of him. Here lie the heroic days of American art, for de Kooning the days of WPA housepainting and commercial art. In 1926 he is snatched from the scene to reappear, younger, in Rotterdam, where he was trained thoroughly, and going back to the ultimate point, 1904, he was born.

Running the movie forward again is to discover in all the de Koonings the sense of crisis projected into the labyrinth of contradictions through which he has zigzagged like a bright planet, holding to small certainties of identity. "I have this sort of feeling that I'm all there now," he told David Sylvester, in sentences that seem clipped and pasted together abruptly from some continuum. "As to the painting being finished, I always have a miserable time over that. But it's getting better now. I just stop."

January 1965
Newsweek

Budd Hopkins: Master of a Movement Manqué

I HAVE a special feeling not for the underdog (who commands universal entropic sentimentality), but for the genuine outsider. Outside the mode, the fashion, the style, the beat. Now that most people cut notches on themselves to measure how far they are "in," the outsider—indifferent to this chic in-out dialectic—is of even more importance. This is what attracted me to Budd Hopkins' work when I first saw it in 1963. It left a startlingly *complete* after-feeling, in the sense that its specific forms seemed haunted by others which they had excluded. It had its own mixed sound, which at that time seemed to me to fall right into an area that was puzzlingly empty: abstraction growing out of Abstract Expressionist ideas and practice, retaining some of both, while connecting with the past to make possible one kind of future, a future that conventional Abstract Expressionism didn't have. (Typically that period—early sixties— was full of quarrels as to whether Abstract Expressionism was "dead" or not. Its extreme apologists wanted to legislate it as a mode forever. As far as I was concerned it had, in its conventional practice, lost its immediacy and relevance. I was looking for a *transformation* in style, not a continuation.)

At that time the city was full of a young breed of tough guys who thought their certificates of inheritance had been stamped by Pollock and Kline and de Kooning and that the future was theirs by divine right. What happened to them is one of the unwritten tragedies of the New York scene, a sort of *hubris* on Tenth Street (although the lessons of the past should have taught them that third-generation inheritors, speeding down the tracks laid by the big men, always get derailed). Pop culture and Pop art, with its lethal antagonisms to and ironic put-ons of overcommitment, cut them down like Easter Islanders catching the measles. The inheritors of the future suddenly found themselves in a moral squeeze to which they reacted according to their nature. If they were honest, they kept up their way of life and saw those bread-and-butter red stars as often as blue moons. Others tried to graft bits of Pop culture onto their beliefs and (since they had moved from the area of creation to that of recipes) mostly cultivated foolish hybrids. Some simply disinherited themselves and started out again. They started out in a different world. It is their tragedy that a taint always sticks to them, like a boyhood indiscretion in a politician's past. This big squeeze was well on when Hopkins showed in 1963.

Hopkins, steeped in the same heroic Tenth Street environment, didn't misread the Delphic oracles. He speaks of the heroes now with an insight their tragically blinded acolytes will never have. He likes a story Franz Kline used to tell:

Pollock, drunk, was insulting some of the boys at the Cedar Bar. Kline went over to tell him to cool it. Pollock got angry that Kline should tell *him* how to behave. He piled up beer glasses in front of him as if he were going to throw them. Kline lifted his end of the table and tipped them into Pollock's lap. Pollock went ominously to the men's room, cleaned himself up, pulled the door off its hinges coming out (to get attention), roared and slowly stalked Kline. They met in the center of the floor, and Kline, who was stronger, hurled Pollock against the bar, where he hurt his back. Pollock roared again and came back. As they struggled Pollock whispered to Kline, "Not so hard, Franz, not so hard."

Though the times are now rough on such a gun-slinger self-image, it isn't just to be laughed at—it enabled him and others to paint the kind of pictures they did paint; illusions so passionately believed in can become facts.

Hopkins is the only one of the third generation (born around 1930) who heard the "Not so hard." He was able to experience the "abex" (as Alfred Barr shorthands Abstract Expressionist) romantic agony, and then step outside it to correlate it with his own tough quietism. For this is the split that his art arches over in images that are as diverse in means as they are classically unified in mood. This was the main point of the 1963 show, which I called post-Abstract Expressionist because it wasn't in the vein of the young inheritors (who examined each other's brush strokes like tea leaves in a cup). It brought seemingly antipathetic ideas ("Hard Edge" shapes, Expressionist strokes) together. This was what I was tuned in to expect (or recognize), but by this time the hounds and horses were off view-hallooing after the bright new things of Pop. Although I had been fed acres of instantly confected abex mediocrity in 1961 and '62 (which seemed summarized by the serviceable abstraction created with a rolling pin in Jack Gelber's *The Apple* and then auctioned off to the audience right out of the play), I felt, perversely, that the abex potentials for development were being neglected. I was also aware that art in America had been totally subservient to its socioeconomic background—movements were scissored off when the banks closed, or politicians went isolationist, or the mass media jumped on their back. I was hoping for some continuities, not quite satisfied then that Pop, in its ricochet opposition to every abex position, was a genuine continuity.

Hopkins wrote about this development—in 1960—before he was able to paint it. "Art is the visual expression of the painter's sense of life. At its deepest it is the harmonious combination of the artist's final dream and his sense of reality. And if this involves contradictory feelings, everything must finally be harmonized and

93

serene." Hopkins' delicate suturing of opposites comes from his genetic imprints, from temperamental necessity. The rest of this statement is full of good things and is worth quoting. "I work for clarity and precision, yet the painting must finally be mysterious and indefinable. It must express structure, order, the marks of overall controlling intelligence, yet it must be alive, free, spontaneous—the ruled edge and the improvised, accidental line, together and harmonized. I like neither extreme in art wholeheartedly, neither the purified world of geometrical art nor the free, indulgent world of Expressionism.

"There is a central tradition in modern art. It is based solidly on Cézanne (not Monet) and includes within it most of Cubism, the great, structured early Matisses, and some of the recent American abstract painting. The art in this tradition is *whole*, yet ultimately serene, precise, harmonious. These are goals I have set for myself."

The work up to this time (1960) is full of the voices of the gods—Guston (delicate knottings and knittings), Kline (large thunderous areas of force), de Kooning (color, and the sense of the loaded brush dragging, flashing, studying its own trail). For all its ventriloquized romanticism, this amalgam is a disguise. For insistent hard edges briefly line themselves up against free rhythms, check a movement, potentially splinter it, and sometimes, by sharpening an edge, cut and tilt an area into another kind of space ("Avalar," 1960, or "Lasemann," 1958). (Guston noticed these ambiguities in Hopkins' 1959 show at Zabriskie and mentioned them to him.) These contrary spatial signals, in their checks and hesitations, give notice that his art was struggling, like an organism, to divide itself and grow through diversity into another kind of unity. It is not surprising that the 1963 show has actual letters jelled in the midst of the pictures' motions and rotations, letters as *objects* which, as with some early Cubists and with Stuart Davis, are signs of composite and contradictory ideas being worked out side by side.

I still think of this development in Hopkins around 1963 as part of an aborted movement, a quiet bit of artistic technology that many artists were testing when the Pop men rushed through the studios, propelled by the unstoppable force of history—and of course most people can't refuse joining a crowd rushing to a happy appointment with both destiny and chic.

Perhaps the prototype of the particular development I mean is in some of Hans Hofmann's paintings in the Kootz exhibition of January 1962. In this show he experimented (though that's rather the wrong word for Hofmann, who made even his mistakes with radiant conviction) with textured, luminous rectangles anchored in Expressionist strokes, an intention later carried to spectacular success. It is hard now, though only a few years have passed, to understand the daring of introducing contrary linear elements, with their superficial connotations of stability, order, purism, into the abex flux. Actually, it was an admission of history, a looking around the monolithic exclusivity of abex and thus, by implication, routing it to a siding while making connections with the past.

It had been done before—like most things in modern art, you can find a precedent if you search, although many people don't realize that the very search is in itself an action defining the new, not showing it up as old stuff in drag—although in a way every innovation is more or less old stuff in drag. (A rapid sketch of precedent would include Renoir's classical hang-up and the hard-edge/soft-stroke dichotomy it provoked; also Kandinsky's transitional phase from Expressionist stroke to sharply defined shapes.) But what gave it its particular savor in the early sixties was the immediate Abstract Expressionist context, the specific "permissions" of that context it exceeded.

Following this idea, I looked around for other artists who seemed to be doing the same thing. Frank Roth was—sort of. In group shows I happened across canvases by Robert Ryman which initiated a dialogue between brushstroke (treated with objectlike impersonality) and geometry—but he abandoned this idea after a few pictures. Later I found that Albert Brunelle, in 1962, had done

95

some excellent work of this nature, had shown it to nobody, and then discarded it as he went on to the idea then becoming dominant—of art as an invention that works. As a movement it seemed stilled before it had really got itself born (although one could read Al Held's cinemascope geometry drawn into lumpy, thick surfaces, as fulfilling its criteria).

So Hopkins' new show* was fascinating for carrying these ideas through to a conclusion, demonstrating one possibility of what that movement might have been. The scumbles and strokes are less frequent than in the 1963 show, their sum of energy exactly measured (as in Gottlieb's later calligraphs) so that this free element can be manipulated as a unit, i.e., as an object or shape among other objects and shapes. Sometimes paint fans out from geometric edges, like snow whipping off an Alp (and rather like Norman Bluhm's white curtains). The flatness of the canvas is deeply compromised by tilts in the planar geometry that, bending it in and out, creating open corners and flanges, produce almost shaped-canvas effects. Some of these geometric shapes are "arbitrary," as some of the shapes in the "new" simplified sculpture (whose precedents are in painting) are arbitrary—once a kiss-of-death word now complimentary and almost synonymous with invention.

Take the white, bifurcated pennant in "Strike White" and you can see how, interlocking with the yellows, stresses and warps are placed on it so that the picture, lifted by those landscape blacks, zigzags in and out like a carefully adjusted spatial concertina. Along the edges, starts and flares of light and dark suspend and accentuate the action, which is stabilized by a red at the right lower corner. In "Strike Blue" there is a deep diagonal cleavage from top right to lower left that tries to fold the picture over—again diverted by staccato darks and lights clicking leftward at a different tempo from that of the yellow shape above, which majesti-

* At the Poindexter gallery, New York, February 11–March 12, 1966.

cally flares out in a smooth move leftward, too. You can pick out the same deep spatial fissures and turntable twists in "Yarmouth" and "Granada." Occasionally (e.g. "Chicago") the plane geometry creates an abstract stage-space in which a spatter of strokes makes a sharply focused gesture, spontaneous and studied, like an actor's. If you examine this seemingly free patch of Expressionism you can see how carefully the strokes mask within them a structure which shifts planes in an echo of the hard surrounding shapes. In contrast to this main preoccupation with illusory violations of flatness, a few of the pictures are flat as diagrams, all consciously set on one tissue-paper-thin plane, e.g., "Red August."

Color shows a somewhat parallel division. Sweet contrasts (usually of yellow and light blue) play against sour off-key dissonances (usually between green-red-dark blue contiguities) which produce a feeling rather like that of chalk grating on blackboard. In summary, the change seems to be from the classic balances of the 1963 show to rather mannered ambiguities that superficially cancel the classical idea. Yet the final effect is mainly one of repose and solution, the feeling of "both familiar and new" maintained, as he wants them to be, simultaneously. What Hopkins is doing with his planar shifts from frontality, sweet and sour color, his Expressionist residue mixing it up with "purist" vocabularies of line and curve, is using mannerist complexities to arrive at resolutions that are still classical, though the means that produce them are not. The end result is thus slightly jarred off, slightly unfocused by this odd relation of means and end.

The corollary of this also holds for a few of the oddest pictures that present themselves as straight and symmetrical when in fact they are cunningly skewed off symmetry. The "Red Emblem Painting" (a black cross hung lozengewise that seems like a design for 1984 armbands—rather like a stripped-down version of Marsden Hartley's "German Officer" series) and "Tarlac" are classicially simple and appear to present audacious symmetries. Yet these are the ones that finally refuse to "solve" themselves and settle into classic

97

repose. This brings one into the currently very active area of ambiguous masking of purist devices, where, instead of being absolutes, the squares, circles, triangles, etc., are surrounded by adjuncts and attitudes that mobilize them into units as personal as brushstrokes under the geometer's disguise. Peter Hutchinson, in a provocative article, has introduced this idea of using classical simplicities to express mannerist distortions. "The contemporary mannerist attempts," he writes, "in seemingly classical work, to make us reconsider purism . . . abstract mannerism can be extremely complicated while maintaining an outward simplicity. The complication is inferred, intellectual, where in previous mannerist work it often was expressed as detail."

This development in Hopkins' work—mannerist modes producing classical, slightly romantic, resolutions, or else classical modes finally producing unrest—is exactly the kind of traffic through a psychological mid-point of intersection that could be expected from one who constantly plays the extremes against the center, who commits one part of himself totally but reserves another part of himself to check constantly on his position. Hopkins' firm control of these precarious variables is the end result of an unusually consistent growth. His path runs from abex to sometimes parallel certain cool ambiguities and shapes of the present, and that progress is logical every step of the way. It's about the only route of that particular kind there is—a path, beaten through the undergrowth of a very real jungle, that never became a smooth macadamed highway.

It is for this essential honesty that I like Hopkins—a cagey enthusiast whose ambitions are subjected to complete inner directional control. He is not the sort of fellow you are going to read about in the glossy columns where kookiness and personal charades are the usual price of admission. This is a good thing. His art is self-protected from all that while it quietly creates a system of values of its own, values that can't easily be taken away from it.

April 1966
Arts Magazine

Morton Feldman

MORTON FELDMAN is a large, beaming man with thick lenses, a sort of dainty, lumbering enthusiasm and a restlessness that urges him to clamber all over the place as he talks to you in his downtown Lexington Avenue apartment.

Clockwise from the door, the walls of that apartment are covered by Vicente, Guston, Guston, Guston, Kline, Rauschenberg, Johns, Guston, Guston, Kline. Feldman doesn't have a de Kooning, but he has a phrase de Kooning once gave away: "I work—other people call it art."

"To me that was the beginning of my life," said Feldman, meaning his musical life, to which, he says, artists have contributed more than musicians. Their ideas and example showed him and some others how to break out of the straitjacket of musical tradition without walking off into a vacuum.

Philip Guston, a close friend, helped him to the idea of sound as a medium to use and abuse like paint. The medium itself should not be sanctified. "Phil Guston took away the initial morality of the medium. 'What am I working with?' he said. 'It's only colored dirt.' I learned one had to make one's own morality—the material itself wasn't an intrinsic moral—like the sonata form. He made the 'I' the material. So he showed me where the responsibility was—not to any 'style,' to any historical vested interest of means."

Guston's "Attar," a tickle of rosy colors threading in and out of a fragrant space, was leaning against the fireplace. Sitting in front of it he pointed one finger at it, another at a ruled orchestral score, finding parallels.

"To me this score is my canvas, this is my space. What I do is try to sensitize this area—this time-space. The reality of clock-time comes later in performance, but not in the making of the composition. In the making of a composition the time is frozen. The time-structure is more or less in vision before I begin . . . I know I need eight or ten minutes like an artist needs five yards of canvas."

His finger hopped around on the spread-out score, honeycombed with alternatives. "I can start here or there—wherever the point is I want to work in or around or from." He pointed to another score that looked like a crossword puzzle by Mondrian. "Each box has a number, the number of sounds that instrument plays on or *within* the duration—that's up to the instrumentalist. I don't tell him the note to play either—just a general area of sound. Since he can place it anywhere in the duration of the box, this means infinite variation of the same quality. Not the same *tune*. You used to have theme and variations. Now you have *quality* and variations.

"What I do is sensitize the whole thing," he went on, "and then I tie it together. It's like a painter. What's a painter got? Form and amounts—"

"Amounts?"

"—touch, frequency, intensity, density, ratio, color." He worked with the Guston as he talked. "It's just the spatial relationship and the density of the sounds that matter—any note will do as long as it's in the register."

"But it'll sound different each time."

"Yes," he said intensely, "but it'll have the same quality, a feeling of density." Ideally, apparently, the piece will have a discipline that will give it identity, and a freedom that will make each performance a new function of that identity, giving the composition, like an action painter's motif, a life of its own.

In fact, the parallel with Abstract Expressionist theory is fairly exact: (1) A motif or quality indivisibly associated with the self, the "I"; (2) a mode of discipline in freedom that substitutes another kind of formal necessity for tradition; (3) the capacity for infinite variations within that discipline while preserving the essential "quality" or "I-ness" of the picture.

What was the relationship of the visual element to the sound when he was composing? "All I can say is that sometimes it doesn't look right visually and then there's something wrong with the whole sound conception. It's as if the rightness of the sound is right visually. It's a simultaneous thing. I don't think of it. It's awfully hard for me to analyze it—I'm anti-process," he said, surprisingly. "I'm always burning the process behind me. I don't like there to be a trace of process in the finished work. I try to begin and work and end without feeling there's a possibility of possibilities." Here is where he abandons the element of choice within which the action painter finds his tension, his constant countering and canceling of possibilities. But musically what he wants to annihilate are the safe variations composers go through like wind-up dolls. "Process," he said, having difficulty now, "disappears in experience, in me." Which brought us to the "I" again, that mysterious "I."

"I don't mean it as the automatic or surrealist 'I,'" he said. I mean somehow the omnipotent 'I.' "

He means an identity that is a sort of grown-up surrealist "I"— one that extends experience, balancing inside and outside, subjective and objective, discipline and freedom in a way that makes his music a sort of living sound-object, a motif in time, the silence of the white canvas painted with sound.

Like the action painters, he makes one aware of his medium as if it were a substance. Silence and intervals have different tensions and structure, created by the sounds that blurt and spray and slip around them. Attention switches from silence to sound and back again in a way reminiscent of figure-ground relationships in the painting he admires. To a conventional musician, his work must often seem like the forms of random choice. To a painter, aware of the disciplines against which he creates tension, his music makes sense.

February 1964
The New York Times

Ad Reinhardt: Anti-Avant-Gardist

"THE absolute in art is absolute."
"Explanation in art is no explanation."
"The invisibility of art is visible."
"Chutzbah [sic] in art is chutzbah."

Ad Reinhardt, now fifty-three, has subjected himself to the glare of a retrospective exhibition at the Jewish Museum and it helps illuminate more clearly the polemics and paradoxes with which he gratefully embalms his art. The embalming process, conducted over the years through a sort of linguistic analysis of what art isn't, has been ruthlessly effective. He has got art where he wants it, related to itself and nothing else.

Thus Reinhardt has pioneered a way of making art you have difficulty writing about. His absolutism includes a hostility toward criticism, since art and verbal symbols are entirely different things (though he himself uses words with great acuteness). He makes such devices as symbol and metaphor appear silly, and sidetracks such standard modes of approach as comparison, stylistic analysis, and formal history. His work subverts, less efficiently, scholastic analysis of his absolute, ideas of transubstantiation and alchemy (modes of conversion of base material into higher status symbolically or actually), and the obvious models provided by Oriental thought. Once he forces critics to accept his very plausible terms, they have to invent a way of writing about him or shut up. It is difficult to separate his actual paintings from the tremendous polemical field of force that surrounds them, constantly drawing attention to the magnitude of his rejections. If strength of will and force of personality are aesthetic qualities, Reinhardt is the greatest of modern masters.

This retrospective is, ironically, due to Reinhardt's emergence in the mid-sixties as an *eminence grise* of Minimal art and tends to elect him to the status of "precursor"—thus subscribing to the idea of formal genealogy, of stylistic cause and effect, which Reinhardt would completely reject. However, circumstances or historical inevitability have provided him if not with issue, at least with fellow spirits—the young monochrome artists and the reductionists who inexhaustibly permute ideas of modular structure. There is a certain touching quality in the spectacle of Reinhardt's justification and triumph—which his own ideas at the same time command him to forego.

There are easy pitfalls in identifying Reinhardt with the new generation. His ties with the generation of the late forties and early fifties are just as impressive, if you care to tease them out. One of his most obvious ties to the new generation is his relation to the audience. A mark of current art is the way in which it builds in self-protection from the ignorant; there is a frequent invitation to boredom, which most of the audience accepts and moves on. (The other protective device is the new cliché of making art that doesn't look like art, but simply like "something or other.") Reinhardt, in turn, literally "screens" his audience by detaining them until their eyes adapt to his dull, nubby surfaces, psychologically putting them in a sort of profane *cella*. (One could write profitably about his cunning subversion of distinct vision in terms of plain physiology here—the eyes' rods and cones being gradually forced into a curious dialogue between edge and surface, acuity and blindness. Sometimes he produces a response without a stimulus.) Waiting for dark-adaption involves a duration demanding an act of will from the spectator, and this interval of sensory deprivation is imposed with considerable power and egotism.

Once this probationary period is over (aesthetics quickly become ethics with Reinhardt. A gnomism his art completely rejects is the one that goes: "The morality of art is not morality." Reinhardt is a relentless moralist), his pictures' surfaces exert a magnetic fascination. The viewer's effort after meaning becomes intense;

while appearing to ignore the viewer, Reinhardt is a complete virtuoso in stage-managing his eye. The more visible paintings, which declare their formularized structure too easily, and which the eye can check rapidly, tend to be easily exhaustible. A lot of the time Reinhardt's art is *too* visible. The best work engages in a serial disclosure of its structure, which is mentally "added up" edge by edge and surface by surface to contribute to the *concept* of its structure. This concept then informs the actual perception which seems, for reasons of shine, lighting, paint absorption, etc., to remain always partial. Thus the picture becomes virtually a thought, latent in the picture, manifest in the mind. There is a marked discrepancy here between the ambiguity inherent in partial perceptions and the absolute formal idea which these perceptions tend to add up to in the mind. This, I think, is the essential nature of Reinhardt's artistic identity: the maintenance of an absolute by ambiguous means—an ambiguity that he almost convinces us doesn't exist in his work. By Reinhardt's canons, the more visible pictures should be his most successful. The ones that in effect fulfill these canons do so by, in fact, transgressing them.

How he gets his pictures to stay at this state of absolute zero is a lesson in how to separate *qualities* and paralyze them with a sort of negative potential. His qualities separate out into the basic vocabulary of any visual stimulus: shape, size, scale, edges, surface, composition, visibility (already it feels as if one were talking in scholastic terms about the properties of a phenomenal object). The predominant five-by-five-foot-square canvas is, whatever disclaimers may be advanced, a very human scale, which doesn't mean the impulse toward it is humanistic. Rather it implies the careful fixing of a stimulus at the median percentile for the size of the creature that will perceive it. (Bigness is stigmatized as rhetoric: "Large sizes are aggressive, positivist, intemperate, venal and graceless.") Light is deposited on his surfaces in a cold grudging fashion—it contracts rather than expands. The canvas is turned so that the horizontal weave is emphasized (like the lines of radioed moon photos), and the illusory loss of surface is canceled as you get close. Closely valued edges are slightly sawtoothed, just enough to advance the idea of an edge to the perceiver. His typical cruciform composition, by not interrupting the horizontal band, refuses the gestalt identification of "cross" and remains particulate. (One of his earlier vertical series demonstrates how to discredit the pillar-shape, just as his huge early red painting shows how to subvert a purist composition by Op color.)

Thus a process of subversion keeps colors and shapes barely contiguous—composition doesn't function as composition, geometry isn't geometry, surface is dissociated from illusion, edges are areas of low tension. What Reinhardt has achieved is a sort of painting that functions like anti-matter to other painting, a complete mirror image (not the opposite) of what other artists would consider painting to be. Expression becomes anti-expression; originality, anti-originality. By a choice set of the most delicately adjusted negatives, he reduces the picture to an illusion of complete stasis. This is not nihilism; its polemical thrust is never toward destruction or a sense of impasse.

In this regard it is interesting to compare Reinhardt's ultimate five-by-fives with Frank Stella's famous exhibition, at Castelli's in 1964, of plum-colored canvases with the centers punched out, an exhibition that has had an immense influence on the younger artists. Here the attack on art history, on criticism, and even on art itself was infinitely more polemical and violent, the personality more acidulous and aggressive. Stella reacted from this position as if, after destroying art history and the expectation of what art should be, he was free to make art once more—which he is currently doing with all his irritating brilliance. Reinhardt's work, for all its polemics, is never nihilistic in the sense that Stella's exhibition was. For Reinhardt always upholds the negatively defined concept of what constitutes art. People who call him nihilistic confuse his means with his end. His art attacks not art, but concepts of art history, and indeed of history, and so, confounding the idea of development, announces another concept of nonlinear time. This demands another kind of criticism, and the challenge to write it has been brilliantly met by Lucy R. Lippard in her catalogue essay.

Since Reinhardt discredits the idea of development, his own development as an artist, laid out in this exhibition over thirty years, seems to reproach him. His desire for justification or explication is thus probably something he gave into against his better judgment, and one finds oneself in the peculiar position of criticizing someone for having a retrospective, when his final, total, static image completely discredits the idea of retrospectives in general.

Finally, I like the image, and the framework it provides, of Reinhardt as an epicurean psychologist drawing up a relationship between a visual stimulus and a creature. He has minimized his stimulus, turned it down to the point where, to follow the psychological image, the signal-noise ratio is almost unitary, where the creature's knowledge of the stimulus is constantly confounded by the visual static on his own receptors as the stimulus approaches silence. If one wished to examine this stimulus, to turn it up and magnify it for analysis, one would find, I think, that Reinhardt has not reduced art to its limits. He has reduced visibility to its limits. His pictures are made against the conventions he would seem to be attacking—relationships, movement, illusion—and their mirrored stasis would clearly register, were our receptor mechanisms more sensitive. But he has almost completely subverted this, and so can preserve the idea of providing one-at-a-time art stimuli for superior members of a rapidly multiplying species.

January 1967
Art and Artists

4. THE NEW MAKERS

Pop at First Sight

IT'S MAD, MAD, wonderfully mad. It's also (at different times) glad, bad, and sad, and it may be a fad. It is called "New Realism," and it opens today at 4 P.M. in the Sidney Janis Gallery.

The occasion is a rear-guard action by the advance guard against mass culture—the mass culture that pushes the individual below the line into the lowest common denominator. In fact, it might be called an artful attempt to enrich spiritual poverty.

Included are advertisements, cutouts, garden tools, a lawn mower, newspapers, toothy Madison Avenue smiles, a refrigerator, cosmetics, plaster pastries—almost everything to assuage all appetites and nothing that you wouldn't see if you watched television commercials from 7 A.M. to 3 A.M.

All these defenseless objects are isolated, surrounded, manipulated in attempts to divert them from their everyday function to aesthetic ends. Here form follows malfunction.

To turn these numb and blunted weapons of industry back on their source, the exhibitors (the word "artist" would require redefinition for use here) make use of the standard ploys of an educated minority against a majority they indulgently despise—they use wit, satire, irony, parody, all the divisions of humor. The exhibitors have a great advantage: the target is known to them and to their audience. The target is so big it's hard to miss.

The general tone is zippingly humorous, audaciously brash, making use of the industrial products of conformity in order to non-conform. Behind this satiric attack on Madison Avenue there stands the injured shadow of the Common Man, sadly using after-shave lotion and brushing his teeth after every meal.

Although the standard vocabulary of such antique art movements as Surrealism and Dada is used, the intent is entirely different: a fresh wind is blowing across the vast billboard wasteland, and anarchy is out.

In Mr. Janis' definition of the "New Realist" art, the touchstone is the "daily object" so manipulated that aesthetic emotion is allowed to replace functional usage.

Although he does not keep strictly to his own definition (anyway, it doesn't seem necessary to establish rigid cut-off points here) he has produced what must be the year's most entertaining show. "Entertaining" is the right word, for the show does not often transcend visual social comment, a sort of red, blue, and yellow journalism.

This is one of the most interesting developments in the galleries, for it marks the entrance of artists into social criticism with ephemeral works that can be thrown away when circumstance has changed enough to remove their relevance. America has been a pioneer in throwaway cups and saucers, milk containers and tablecloths. Now it is a pioneer in throwaway art.

It might be added here that the articles in the catalogue take this development very seriously. "Pop" art, a very good name, becomes "New Realism." Since the very essence of the movement is compounded of lightness, irreverence, and wit, it would be ridiculous to take it with deep philosophical seriousness. This would perform the nice trick of making mass culture esoteric.

Not all the show is lightweight (just as not all the show is American—there is good work from Britain and the Continent). But the clever things hook the eye. A dancing board shows the steps of a fox-trot. A rack of supermarket supplies is carefully compartmented. A la billboard hoardings, there is a vast painted eye. There's also the old package trick—a package bound up with cord, with the permanent promise of unopened goods. There are papier-mâché pastries. All these are smart one-shot rockets that have no second stage.

What is welcome is a higher sense of aesthetic responsibility among a few whose work has been turning up this year. Andy Warhol (despite his "Fox Trot"); Jim Dine, who goes past banality to produce some strange, seriously disturbing pieces, including a dislocating bathroom board with mirror, toothbrush and soap dish; Tom Wesselmann, who parodies bright advertisements until they become slightly cuckoo, and, of course, Wayne Thiebaud. The excellent work by foreign artists is more traditional in style. The main interest is the American satire of America's mass market—this is new. The find of the exhibition is George Segal, whose white lifesize figures set up in hollow tableaux are as memorable and upsetting as stumbling into a ghost town dusted with fallout.

With this show, Pop is officially here. It is, of course, founded on the premise that mass culture is bad, an expression of spiritual poverty. So perhaps this is the old story of the avant-garde given the opportunity to seize on the bourgeois again, this time through their packaged products. Or, more amusingly, things may have reversed themselves, and now it may be the bourgeois that shocks the avant-garde.

October 1962
The New York Times

Words: An Environment

"Say, did you see this Happening?"
"What Happening?"
"Words."
"Words?"

"That's what it's called—'Environment: Words'. It's at Smolin's."

"Off-Madison?"

"Right. Well, you go into this little room, and all around is words, just words."

"Words?"

"Yeah, like a holiday for nonverbals. Words are written on the walls. You can hardly see the wall for the words."

"What words?"

"Any words; that's part of it—any word like 'bang' or 'Hitler' or 'call.' "

"I get it—just words."

"Right. Like a random sample. Exploiting the laws of chance, see?"

"The subconscious?"

"No, no, no. How can I get it to you? Happenings are governed by laws of chance, and with permutations of the variables the possibilities are endless—while they still have the authority of law. Get it?"

"OK. What else?"

"There are these lights, see? Red and white lights going off and on."

"Why?"

"Well, that's the time element measured visually instead of audibly as in the tick of a clock. Then there's a ladder. You can move it around. Climb it. Add your own word. There's room at the top. You don't dig?"

"No."

"OK, listen to this. Here's a guy writing about it. 'Mr. Allen Kaprow'—that's the artist—'surrounds us with an environment of unrelated words, illuminated by intermittent lights, augmented by recordings of verbal and nonverbal poems the visitor can manipu-late—' "

"There are records too?"

"Yeah, but listen: 'The comment is made through confusion, the tension created by the meaning of the words in their meaningless setting. The isolated barbs of meaning attack the participant to make him a sort of modern, word-struck Sebastian. They finally induce an emotional aphasia—' "

"What's aphasia?"

"Who cares? Look it up."

"Tell me more."

"Well, in our society some words are used more and more like a sort of Poisson distribution. Words that are used more and more mean less and less—primary words like 'love' and 'God' and 'war' and 'abstract'—"

"OK, I get it. What next?"

"Now you go into the next little room."

"Why?"

"A sign tells you—a direct order, an unambiguous proposition, an oasis of meaning. Now you go in. This is where you can really join in. There are these ribbon streamers hanging from the ceiling. And pieces of chalk and lipstick. And squares of paper on a hook. You can take a piece of paper, see—and write, and pin your note on a streamer. Or if you feel like it you can write on the wall."

"What's written on the squares of paper?"

"All sorts of things. Like 'Call Jim, Jenny, he's back,' and 'Michelle, see you at George's noon Friday—R.' and things like that."

"But this happens all the time. People write notes all the time."

"But not this way."

"I guess that's true. What did you write?"

"Me? I wrote S–M–O–G, ve—e—ery slow, in red chalk. On the wall."

"Why?"

"I just felt like it. I didn't know what I was going to write. It just happened. It was a terrific experience. Just as if I were writing a solution of an equation of probability."

"Did you feel better?"

"Not better. Different. This guy Kaprow's got something. You should go see this show."

"Yes, but what's it got to do with art?"

"Who cares? Go."

September 1962
The New York Times

Robert Rauschenberg I

THE most obstreperous creation in Robert Rauschenberg's large retrospective exhibition at the Jewish Museum is something called "Broadcast" (1959), which accompanies the spectator everywhere with cacophonous sounds. The noise is transmitted from behind the picture surface by three radios tuned to a single control. Twist the control knob and you come up with three new stations, randomly selecting odd combinations of Pop music, newscasts and static. The auditory image is of overcrowded wavelengths choking in their hurry to feed the masses.

The scrambled sound blares from behind a typical Rauschenberg collage, combining slashes of paint, a piece of comb, the word HELP, and news photos of such mass diversions as a horse race, the city, a police beating. From close up, the photos demand individual attention. As you move out they blend into a visual delirium that matches the sound, and as you withdraw further, they sink into a strong abstraction that swings in its own way.

Obviously a new era is at hand. If you can't lick the environment, join it. For many years Rauschenberg has been pointing steadily toward an annihilation of conventions in a new freedom. His main characteristic is a conquest of common everyday reality from a bridgehead of Abstract Expressionism. He is trying to materialize an ambiguous limbo between high art and low life. His "combines," as he calls them, are on the crest of a new popular wave they helped to start. At thirty-eight, Rauschenberg is both contemporary and historical, and his creations tend to force a redefinition of what art is all about.

As in much modern art, his work makes the common distinction between painting and sculpture outdated. Combining sound, flashing lights (and occasionally movement) with hand painting, his pieces aspire to the dimension of time, and thus performance. The collage materials are lovingly gathered from the encounters of real life—he has a fondness for such rejects as old tires, old newsprint, old clothes. As if in tribute to the Unknown Bum, this flotsam is battered by time and the anonymous hands that have touched it, used it, thrown it away. When everything is put together, the main adhesive force is the anti-logic of the subconscious.

Indeed, it is this that enables him to blaze a road from Abstract Expressionism to Pop. Each of these in its own way draws on Surrealism. Abstract Expressionism found some authority in Surrealist automatism. Pop at its infrequent best depends in part on the shocks produced by free association.

Obviously, if he wanted to, Rauschenberg could be a fine Abstract Expressionist or a fine neo-Dadaist. But the fascinating thing about him is that he seems to feel the need of a new method, a process that swallows life whole and presents it with enough transformation to aspire incidentally to art. In his useful catalogue, Alan R. Solomon draws attention to a crucial quote from Rauschenberg that can be paraphrased: "I try to act in that gap between . . . art and life." Since Rauschenberg's aesthetic digestion is occasionally not strong enough to take care of stuffed fowl and zip fasteners, his work is sometimes defeated by life and rejected by art.

But the general success of his work, invaded by life and aspiring toward art, is most impressive. It is far from being just Dada or Surrealism once more with feeling. It negates nihilism to lay claim to life and its confusions. It implies a respect for an audience and an attempt to meet it—a new development in modern art, also seen in the Happening, a semitheatrical extension of Rauschenberg's performance between life and art.

As distinct from the blank anonymous face of the Pop artist, Rauschenberg decisively retains for himself the personal role of creator. All his work is steeped (sometimes literally) in Abstract Expressionism. Most of his appendages—Coca-Cola bottles, a cock, stuffed birds (some of which had to have hernias repaired by a taxidermist before the show)—are related to, or incorporated into, canvases with a sensibility that of its nature abhors disorder. In everything he does, he feels the lyric pull—and maybe he is too lyric an artist for the rough, tough role of pioneer. Such constructions as "Rhyme," "Wager," and "Hymnal," are exquisite in a way that completely transforms their collage elements. Life is overcome by art. Rauschenberg is a great civilizer of objects, from the torn telephone book in a tabernacle-like inset to Coca-Cola bottles transformed into slim, elegant presences. His sensibility and his sense of revolution are at odds in the failures, and they pull together in the total successes. In his most individual and interesting work they fight, occupying his chosen gap between life and art.

His use of collage elements, especially news photos, can be confusing. From a distance they are drowned in total abstraction. Up close, they often refuse to settle in, selfishly declaring their individuality. Although chosen by Rauschenberg during meaningful encounters, their obvious meaning (or lack of it in their present situation) can be disturbing. Perhaps, as the general trend of his work indicates, they are part of an attempt to come in contact with indubitable bits of reality, which become lost in the flux of abstraction as one retreats from the work.

Thus, perhaps Rauschenberg marries two realities—abstract energy with its connotations of the unseen, as in physics, and the fragment that has an obvious relevance to everyday life. This is an ambiguity shared by us as we live, as well as by Rauschenberg's constructions. Such an explanation gives authority to his work if it does not justify it on current aesthetic grounds. But it is a measure of his performance that it brings up the question of the redefinition of these grounds.

Rauschenberg is one of the most fascinating artists around. Poised between painting and the object, between art and life, his work is part of a new question thrown at the confused nature of reality, and thus of art.

April 1963
The New York Times

Robert Rauschenberg II

ONE DAY in 1962 Robert Rauschenberg came up to The New York Times, where I was working as a critic. He was looking for discarded photoengraving plates—newspaper detritus that eventually finds its way back into the melting pot. We went upstairs to drawerfuls of dead plates. As he went through them, it became one of those occasions when one understands an artist profoundly.

Always Rauschenberg has, in the process of living, gathered material for paintings, combines, constructions. The casual encounters are made meaningful by a certain concept which functions like a magnet, drawing to him what he wants, repelling what he doesn't. He has to live the parts (a Coca-Cola bottle, a tire, a rag) before he can divine the relations—an act somewhat like stepping out of one's stream of life (as we all do on occasion) and making a summary before progressing, though this is a rather pretentious way of describing something that for Rauschenberg is supple and natural.

When in 1962 he discovered a method of dealing with photographs—those clipped fractions of raw "reality"—by means of silk screens, he went hunting for the suites of images that have since become famous in his paintings and prints—the radarscopes, the parachutist, the Kennedy photograph, the Statue of Liberty, etc. In photographs the encounters have already taken place through anonymous cameramen, so at the *Times* he could flick through chance compendiums of life like the pages of a book, though the plates were so psychologically loaded they should have been handled like bombs.

Rauschenberg went through some plates more carefully, rejected a map of city streets ("It's already been subjected to thought, or art of a sort"). Which led us to his principle of selection, which seemed, typically, to be a nonprinciple. "It's a very difficult problem to pick and handle one's images, because one self-consciously avoids being conscious of one's own taste. One has to step around that. I'm well aware that the decisions I make in avoiding my own taste are exercising my own taste."

This self-willed paradox becomes very clear when one looks at almost any of his works since 1962. For his selection of images (captionless photographs become twentieth-century anonymous) is consciously nonrelated rather than unconsciously related. "Once I have made a selection of images, I get rid of the image that's closing it into a system—or get three more that broaden it out again. I like images to be as general-looking as possible."

What is in action here is a principle of avoidance that roadblocks those overpopulated surrealist highways ("I hate Surrealism"). The avoidance works out as a system of nonassociations with the separateness kept intact—allowing the entire picture to keep its unity through a separation of the parts. Such was the revolutionary concept he brought in with "Rebus" in 1962. Then the picture aspired through real objects to become an environment. In 1962 came the second stage of his brilliant invention. He used the device of silk-screened photographs to get "real" objects back onto the flat surface—a development no one expected. "I wanted to get it back flat," he says, "to see if I really did have anything, to see if it could stand being flat."

The test is cruelest in the strict straitjacket of black-and-white prints. "It's a very stiff medium," he says. But the process has that off-balance magic that fascinates him. One works in the dark, as it were, and then suddenly the image is there. "I used to do photography and I have the same sense of mystery with lithos. When you're working you're conscious that the stone has got a thin skin and weighs seventy-five or a hundred pounds, and what happens is the result of having worked so *thinly* on such a mass. Then it's paper and ink and you see what you've done. It's like adding two and two and not getting four or five."

The unity and separateness that characterize his surface are visible not only in the separate images, but in the relationship of image to the ink within which it exists. The relationship is often composed of a make-and-break perceptual shift—now we see the stroke, now we see the image (the huge barbless arrows in "Front Roll" have immense physical vitality, then out of the "express" stroke the Statue of Liberty hurtles, foreshortened—and one could analyze the gear-changing mechanism through which each constantly modifies the other). His prints, like the frank perceptual elements in Op art, exist in time but at a more complex level. Then again, the third alternative occurs—the total unity of stroke and image into an object, when he gets a "brushload of paint with an image in it," a full Walt Disney flourish in which the flash of a wide "brush" miraculously leaves a fully formed image in its track.

In his prints this sense of speed, of instant inspiration, is undoubtedly a revolution in handling the litho stone. The stiff tedium of the medium is something Rauschenberg is willing to suffer infinitely for his sudden effect. Inspiration is a strategy, not a frenzy. A picture must be subverted, not made.

"The health of the eye seems to demand an horizon," said Emerson. "The sky meeting the ground," says Rauschenberg, "is a detail we are less familiar with." The characteristics of his art (seen at their highest purity in his twenty prints) are all horizonless—movement, randomness, up and down, oblique thrusts in and out, activity, ceaselessness and renewed surprise. When the surprise exhausts itself—or the viewer—his pictures begin to lose their shock and vitality and are time-broken into brilliant museum art. "The moment a picture begins to look like you think it does," he says, "it's nearly gone." The picture is perishable, as Duchamp says, and as with any organism, what happens to it may add to it, modify it, change it, become a part of it, kill it or revive it. A lethal fracture of the stone two years ago brought one of his great prints to instant life. He called it "Accident," welcoming the collaboration of chance.

The twists and turns of the guy ahead of the pack, the foxy craftiness, the innocence, the saying black is white and making you believe it, the strategies by which he takes on the world in all its multiplicity from the Statue of Liberty to Vietnam, are all part of the answer he comes up with that is true for life as well as for his art—you live in it, but you don't have to understand it. This simple philosophic content has had tremendous influence on the New York art that followed—the anonymous surface, the cool, the elucidations of that principle of irrelevance which he pioneered. He made the key that opened the door to the real world, where the newspaper waits on the doorstep.

May 1965
Catalogue of the VI Exposition Internationale de Gravure,
Ljubljana, Yugoslavia

Morris Louis

MORRIS LOUIS was born the same year as Jackson Pollock— 1912. He died in 1962, and it is only in the last few years that his name has become known even to a limited public. Essentially he was appreciated within the trade—a painter's painter, tackling painter's problems with a complete disregard for anything but these problems—so important to the artist and twentieth-century art, so unintelligible to the public at large. His reputation is justly growing.

That reputation will receive an impetus from the Guggenheim Museum's exhibition of seventeen of his paintings done between 1954 and 1960. They show a different side of the painter who in his last few years created those electric bands of vertical color that brought a new motif and a deeper understanding of color into modern art. The last works tend to leave the surface of the canvas behind as attacking color fights outward toward the eye.

This earlier work is content to stay on the surface and to suggest, with marvelous discretion, a gliding shallow space beneath it. Color is still pure but overlaid in layers and translucencies that mute it, and it blazes briefly, like a flame from a broad wick, only when it runs to an edge.

The actual painting of these canvases is highly original. The superimposed washes of color stain into the canvas, bringing out the grain, so that it takes on a rapt, velvety quality, emphasizing the sense of drifting layers of light trapped and held still. The motifs are often club-shaped, or spray out like fans, or rear up in huge hammerheaded plateaus that are occasionally sliced into fingers. The main point about these pictures is their poetic intensity, an intensity that fixes motifs that would otherwise have a slight uneasiness.

This work relates interestingly to the paintings of Louis' contemporaries. Huge in size, they are really magnified lyrics that seem to show an awareness of Clyfford Still's motifs and Mark Rothko's intense, muted color. In fact, they are a sort of lyric accompaniment to the researches of those quietistic painters in the ambience of Abstract Expressionism, Newman, Rothko, and Still—the Field Painters, as Lawrence Alloway calls them in his catalogue—each of whose paintings, no matter how large, must be seen as a single field, a single perception, or it is meaningless.*

* A misreading of Louis's pedigree, of which I was unaware. Seeing Helen Frankenthaler's stain-painting, "Mountains and Sea" (1952), provided him with what he called "a bridge between Pollock and what was possible."

The work at the Guggenheim is mostly very fine, and shows a growing awareness of the dynamics of pure color and its perception. Gradually, toward the nineteen-sixties, the color intensifies, coming forward more aggressively as if it were going to push the picture out in front of the frame. Optical curiosity subdues the lyricism. The two lower corners of a huge bare canvas of 1960 are saturated with zebra-like markings of pure color, leaving inside a vast empty space while at the corner of each eye the colors snap and clash. And in "White," done around the same time, a magnificent spray of pure colors, none of them the same, fights out of the canvas toward the eye like an onrushing crowd. Here we are anticipating the later Louis, the harsh poet of the single image, the bar of strident, vertical colors. In the last works (not represented here, which is a pity) he seemed to be completing the modern tradition of pure color creating form and yet moving beyond it, for his colors refused to settle in space but kept shivering in a sort of astigmatic disturbance.

It is here that Louis becomes historically fascinating. His earlier work is traditional in its tone, if original in its technique and scale. The lyricism is tender, the sensitivity acute. Later, with the war of the colors, it becomes more urgent, more immediate, as if attacking the color-as-form tradition out of which it grew. Now that tradition, once so domineeringly pervasive, is retreating rapidly.

The work of the fifties is a sort of muted chamber music behind the big guns of that era, and the Guggenheim has done well to bring it to wider attention. It shows Louis gathering himself for the leap into that final phase that may be less complete as art but is more vital and disturbing—as color tears away from the picture surface and from tradition, crowding the eye, forcing ambiguities, bringing the painting right into the eye at any cost. To this the work at the Guggenheim is the restrained and often exquisite prelude.

At his last exhibition at the Emmerich Gallery, in October 1962, one could see his final development of the later phase. Stiff scarves of vibrating color hang usually from the tops of his pictures, isolated against the fine granular surface of the unpainted canvas. Sometimes up to fifteen narrow bands compose these spectrums, the bands rubbing against each other at the lines of junction.

As in his previous exhibition (at the same gallery in October 1961), the bright colors cause some of these spectrums to move in and out like corrugations, or to simulate corrugations, or occasionally to push one strip of color forward in space, putting all the other strips out of focus. Occasionally the line of junction between complementary—or close to complementary—colors seems to come right out of the canvas to slice into the eye like the thin end of a wedge, as happens for instance with the green and red in "Moving In."

By this stage it becomes obvious that Louis' paintings happen more in the eye than on the canvas. Their importance lies in the fact that they precisely define the capacities of the eye to separate, combine, and resolve colors in a sharply controlled situation. Although many will not allow themselves or their eyes to tolerate this investigation, the eye is the organ on which the artist plays. Louis played on it almost like a master.

The final exhibition showed two new developments. Some of the multicolored scarves were tilted to cross the canvas diagonally, like a sort of giant gift wrapping. Since they are now out of the vertical, the strips of color do not jog and jostle the eye as much. They are also less powerful in their effect, and this departure must be described as a test, done just to see how it would look.

The other innovation is that the vertical band occasionally has another smaller band providing a sort of counterpoint to it a short distance away, each relating to the other across an interval of cool, colorless canvas. Louis' method of conjugating his color bands could be called a sort of color grammar. The last works are tighter and more precise, the grammar is more knowing, the conjugations are more controlled. But the colors still pop and spring disturbingly out of the canvas, placing stresses on the eye that shatter contemplation.

This happens so consistently that a jazzy dissonance may have been his aim; the one canvas in which the color does not hop and jump is quite dead. But the active dissonances of color are still at slightly too high a level for the eye to tolerate comfortably.

The flawed perfection of Louis' pictures is a real contribution to the branch of modern art that (to keep up the grammar comparison) gives up the subject completely to keep conjugating the predicate, while ignoring the object. To put it in another way, he follows the great example of those (like Josef Albers, or, less often, Mark Rothko) who measure that fascinating interval between reality (what is actually on the canvas) and appearance (what it looks like). His late paintings become extraordinary stimuli.

September 1963
The New York Times

Roy Lichtenstein: Triumph of Subject

ONE of the worst artists in America has raised some of the most difficult problems in art. The artist is Roy Lichtenstein, whose recent exhibition continued what some might be impolite enough to call his gimmick—Pop paintings based on comic strips and done in a sort of typewriter Pointillism (derived from photoengravings) that laboriously hammers out such moments as a jet shooting down another jet with a big BLAM, and a baseball player scowling because, according to an expert on the gallery floor—a child—"he got hurt and didn't know if he could pitch again." Such matters of iconography aside, Lichtenstein briskly went about making a sow's ear out of a sow's ear. Vacancy is a mode of expression that apparently suits him.

The first argument that fills the vacuum around Lichtenstein's paintings is whether he reproduces his comic-strip originals or whether he transforms them. Lichtenstein experts say his work shows slight differences from the originals (proving that he doesn't transcribe but transforms like a good artist should)—differences it takes a Lichtenstein expert to find.

The question of transformation became acute when Lichtenstein lifted a diagram "explaining" a portrait of Mme. Cézanne from a monograph by Erle Loran, a California professor and abstract artist. Enlarged with mechanical devotion, it became art. Or did it? And the game was on.

It's not a new game. Marcel Duchamp, the old master of innovation, started it all years ago by setting up his ready-mades (a hatrack, a urinal, etc.) and calling them art, leaving on us the burden of proof that they were not. Forty years later, they are definitely part of the history of art. Since then there have been numerous such acts of wicked aplomb, all forcing a definition of art, and all putting stress on the basic idea that art in some way alters or transforms life, nature, reality, or whatever you want to call it. Lichtenstein's art is in the category, I suppose, of the handmade ready-made.

What he has done is put a frame of consciousness around a major part of American life we take for granted (the funnies), fulfilling a criterion students have been writing in their notebooks for years— "Art intensifies one's sense of the world around us."

In fact, his banal work fulfills enough textbook criteria of what art should be to call the criteria into question. The Lichtenstein controversy is really a symptom of a deep unease among critics, historians, and some artists as to what art is all about—a more difficult problem than usual nowadays when anyone with any honesty often has to admit he just doesn't know.

So exactly how does one express a deep conviction that Lichtenstein's work isn't art, or, more important, isn't worthy of becoming so?

Those holding that Lichtenstein transforms his material are wide open. Naturally, his subject matter is beyond attack, since anything can be the subject of art. But the content of a work of art is partly in its attitude, formal or otherwise, to its subject. The best Lichtenstein can do is offer us a deadpan vacuity. His work provokes a double take because nothing could be that empty (it is, which may be a creative achievement of a sort). However, the point is how long banality can represent banality and where it stops.

But when one looks at Lichtenstein's paintings as handmade ready-mades, the problems are much more complex. While, in my opinion, what he does is certainly not art, time may make it so, with a little help from the present. It becomes art through a process that forces the critic outside art as such to become a sort of social critic. For unless one goes around with eyes closed, one cannot help but notice how art of no importance (such as Lichtenstein's) is written about, talked about, sold, forced into social history and thus into the history of taste, where it is next door to acceptance as art. One cannot escape an uneasy sense that for the first time in history, instead of our art choosing us, we are choosing our art. The next question is, "Who does the choosing?"—a question that brings down the Furies, half of them pure believers, the other half, naturally, the vested interests. They elect to choose, denying others the freedom to unchoose. There is something wrong in a process that makes the artist a bystander at a struggle deciding whether his work will qualify or not.

Lichtenstein has produced paintings that carry no inherent scale of value, leaving that value to be determined by how successfully they can be rationalized, tucked into society, and placed in line for the future to assimilate as history, which it shows every sign of doing. A strange convergence of circumstances has enabled Lichtenstein to add an unworthy graft to the body of art. It seems to be taking, and there seems to be nothing one can do to stop it.

October 1963
The New York Times

Frank Stella

FOR YEARS people have been complaining that much modern art is about nothing. Frank Stella's new paintings at Castelli's are so much about nothing they turn lack of meaning into a thesis.

They look like nothing at all—merely triangles, hexagons, and rhomboids of canvas, colored a grainy purple, with concentric yellowish lines repeating these shapes inward to where a triangle, a hexagon or a rhomboid is cut out of the center of the canvas, revealing the wall on which the pictures hang. The paintings thus frame, surround, and focus on—nothing, a rather obvious metaphor. They are done in a neat, clerkish sort of way.

A hypothetical Mass Man invited in from the street would have no difficulty ignoring them. To one aware of the dialectical footwork and history of modern aesthetics, they could mean a lot. Which goes to show that modern art (in some of its forms) is a matter of a simple stimulus throwing a switch on the vast invisible superstructure of ideas the artist's ideal audience has to carry around with it. Art like Mr. Stella's is a matter of initiation, a sort of conundrum. Once you get it, you get something out of it.

Thus it is blankly exclusive to a degree that would be contemptuous if contempt were the aim of these works—which it isn't. Their main characteristic is total indifference. Valueless as art, they are of interest because of the slightly awesome paradoxes they imply, paradoxes relating to a way of art and a way of individual existence. For these paintings are sophisticated refinements of the anti-art (and anti-life) trend that has manifested itself in modern art by sporadic attempts at suicide ever since Dada. Such crudities as indignation and protest—because they recognize something to protest against—are passé. Meaninglessness is an absolute, not a relationship.

Part of the paradox of these pictures is that they seem to affirm the value of art while in fact they destroy it. They have a pallid semi-iconic air, a slight visual impact, a slight, easily satisfied Euclidian curiosity, like etiolated examples of the chart painting in the galleries, of which Stella was a distinguished pioneer. These pictures purposely use a knowledge of art for a sort of self-sterilizing operation. By cutting a void into the center of each canvas, the eye's natural point of focus, they induce a sort of Pavlovian frustration.

At this stage one would be quite entitled to dismiss them as perversions of feeling, as forced emblems of an emotional neutralism. Indeed, when looked on as art, that is exactly what they are: a perversion of the function of art by using its formal repertoire to deny the possibility of feeling.

The point is, however, that these works, like an increasing body of modern art, have ceased to have aesthetic significance, but are significant as a social symptom—something that parallels the breakdown of formal criticism's capacity to deal satisfactorily with art of this nature. As a social symptom one could call these works expressions of disgust at the system that consumes them, condemnations of the people who buy them on the basis of ideas that they (the pictures) no longer support. However, to my mind, these works are expressions of a new spiritual position that is of great interest, even if (paradoxically) the art that transfers it is not. Which, by the way, would make Stella a sort of philosophical journalist expressing ideas in visual terms.

These paintings are semi-icons for a spiritual blank. They make Stella the Oblomov of art, the Cézanne of nihilism, the master of ennui. An excess of objectivity turns his pictures into mere objects, the artist into a conditioned reflex, transforming heaven and hell into a new sort of spiritual vacuum that is modified only by his willingness to share it. Art apparently has nowhere to go but down. What is fascinating about Stella is that, while apparently elevating its powers, he has found a way to depress it further, which is not as easy as it sounds.

Thus his new paintings are unimportant. What is important is that they announce that a new kind of animal is around, a new response to living life—one that is anti-emotion, anti-human, anti-art (by transgressing its limits of expression or nonexpression) and even anti-anti. His pictures illustrate a sort of existential crisis that refuses even the action—or commitment—that will reveal its condition to the self. Stella has used modern art to make the supreme nonstatement. In the midst of the confusion and inverted values of art right now, I suppose that's an achievement of a sort.

January 1964
The New York Times

Marisol: The Enigma of the Self-Image

THE MARISOL EXHIBITION at the Stable Gallery is full of Marisols—plaster Marisols, photographed Marisols, wooden Marisols—and it was being haunted by Marisol herself in person. She drifted around in a loose gray sweater, blue jeans tucked into high boots, touching up her new exhibition—which runs from a huge John Wayne (looking like a male hormone in jackboots) to two monstrous children over seven feet tall, each holding a doll with Marisol's face.

Her exhibition—which marks a giant step forward in her power, subtlety, and seriousness as an artist—is a frozen *Marienbad* full of puzzled self-images at different ages and in different roles. Marisol finds it easier to make art out of herself than to talk about herself. She refuses to join you in contemplation of her own mystery, but remains an island, sometimes distant, sometimes close, according to the conversational weather. But always separate. "Why is my own face one of my preoccupations? Because I can't find out what I look like."

A widely multiplied enigma, Marisol is also an enigma to herself.

127

Sometimes she sees herself sharp-featured and high-fashioned, sometimes blunted and round, the face set in an Egyptian tunnel of hair, occasionally as a woman out walking with four faces looking simultaneously in all directions. Her face is open and yet closed. She keeps her large dark eyes fixed on you. When puzzled she rubs her lower lip with the back of her little finger. Her dialogue is Pinteresque.

"Who do you like?"

"????"

"Artists, I mean?"

"I like them all."

"Do you like Pop?"

"Bob?"

"Pop."

"Yes, I like Pop."

"What beautiful woman do you identify with?"

"With nobody."

"Do you have a sense of humor?"

"Yes."

"Do you like your work interpreted as satire?"

"I don't care what they think." Pause. "I don't think much myself. When I don't think all sort of things come to me."

"What sort of things?"

"Ideas. Like the big babies."

"Did you think of Goya's 'Saturn' when you did them?"

"No."

"Do you ever go mad, break things, use bad language?"

"Very rarely."

"You don't like to talk about your work?"

"I don't know what to say."

"Do you go to much theater?"

"No, I never go. It makes me nervous."

"Do you like movies?"

"Yes."

"*Marienbad?*"

"It is my favorite. I even copied some of the gestures in it, the hand of the man who played with one of the matchboxes. And *Mondo Cane.* That's where I got my dog from." (She has constructed a small dog to accompany four Marisols—three adults, one child—out on a walk.)

All this is much less cool than it sounds, for Marisol is far from deadpan. The questions go inward with an almost physical impact through the extraordinary waiting face with arched nostrils, slim Spanish nose, high cheekbones, all emerging from a streamlined inky wave of hair. It is a face uncovered by her concentration; small subtle changes produce large effects. At times she is as dark and slicingly remote as a bullfighter, sometimes vulnerably female, and when she smiles it is like watching someone come out of a tunnel. Since words seem to be a form of direct experience that is painful to her, conversation with her is an extraordinarily bare experience. Like Jeanne Moreau, she frequently has one of the great properties of the legend-provoking female—the magnetic asexuality of an extraordinarily beautiful woman who makes absolutely no concessions to her beauty.

Marisol's vital statistics are sparse. She was born in Paris thirty-three years ago and has been traveling since. Her childhood was spent in Europe and Venezuela. Her parents were "business people"; they had nothing to do with art. She has one brother, an economist. She doesn't like Venezuela or Europe, where she spent eighteen months in Rome. She has never been to Spain because she thought it would be like Venezuela. She came to New York in 1950, went briefly to the Art Students League and then to Hans Hofmann.

"How did you paint then?"

"Like a Hans Hofmann student. The sculpture? I picked it up on my own."

Her virtuosity is astonishing. The show is a compendium of people (her friends, including Andy Warhol), environments and events—people dancing, out for an automobile ride, at a restaurant with food painted onto the table, a wedding, with Marisol—the bride—marrying Marisol—the bridegroom. One can assemble a catalogue of real objects—lots of shoes, a couch, a handbag, a mandolin, saxophone and trumpet from a jazz group with a vague cousinship to Picasso's "Three Musicians." Everything has been hauled into a sawed-up, hammered world where reality and abstraction, objects and their painted images, statement and suggestion, all lock into a solid kaleidoscope in which her face appears and disappears like a mute obsession, never smiling, a mystery like Garbo.

Watching her going through her exhibition, constantly meeting her own image, I asked her if she had ever met her *Doppelgänger*, that ghostly projection of oneself that can meet one face to face.

At last she said, "I saw myself once, one evening when lying in bed, a shadow flying through the air, like a silhouette, a cutout, front face."

"Were you terrified?"

"Yes."

March 1964
The New York Times

Lindner's Private but Very Modern Hades

"When I don't paint," says Richard Lindner, a small, spare sixty-three-year-old with alert features and a tonsured head, "I have a psychological problem. When I paint it's a kind of emotional execution."

Each of his strange paintings at Cordier and Ekstrom's can be looked on in that way—emotional executions or catharses resolving a dense network of psychological relationships so that they can regroup themselves and build up tension again.

His pictures look like no one else's. The women are clumsy

Valkyries stuffed into the elasticized trappings of female hardware. The underwear is dissected with a fixation that becomes symbolism in art, and in life a form of fetishism. Men are more neutral. Over-stuffed children slide into sight like fat moons. Occasionally animals float around, released from gravity.

Also moving into this suspended world, swinging it into balances and counterbalances like some clockwork mechanism, are clusters of pure abstraction. Its hard sharp colors are part of an environment with which the figures must cope. Like materialized ideas, it obliter-ates an eye with a target, cuts into a figure, turning part of it into an arbitrary stylization, like a robot. And everything is shuffled in a trick cardboard space like a cubicle that got rotated and slid into an overlapping semi-Cubist limbo.

Such diverse elements stay together because they seem directly projected from the subconscious through an eye that defines every-thing as sharply as a lens, giving a precision as if the subconscious were being examined in a laboratory. The Herculean mannerism would be vulgar if it were not perfectly fastidious, like watching a heavy, rather indigestible meal eaten with the best of manners.

What Lindner has done is to revivify Surrealism by emancipating it from its past, finding new ways of stating old dilemmas of person-ality—which is in itself a definition of originality—by using both past and present to contribute to his synthesis.

Léger, of course, is very much present. Equally, or perhaps more so, is one of the most unappreciated of artists, Oskar Schlemmer, whose dispassionate analysis of human figures into robotlike pat-terns is such an essential part of Lindner's work. He shows a rare willingness to learn from his juniors—the color of the new abstrac-tion frequently slices its electrified edges through his pictures, and more and more they contain the mass motifs of Pop.

But over and above all this, something else, something archaic, nags you until you have to abandon painting altogether. For his atmosphere becomes more and more reminiscent of *The Cabinet of Dr. Caligari,* his women of Marlene Dietrich in *The Blue Angel—*

movies that went deep during his childhood in Nuremberg. All these sources are fused and sustained by the purity of obsession to make mute concentrations of inaccessible meaning.

Whatever its deeper meanings, this theme is the elaboration of the gross and subtle tensions between a number of human and inhuman equations. He explores pungently the relationships of men to women, adults to children, animals to people, and abstraction to all these varieties of life. The meaning is never manifest, but latent in carefully bizarre juxtapositions.

Another relationship is being defined in the present show—between the subconscious and the world around, between the extremely personal and the extremely public. His pictures have developed an appetite for flags, tiger motifs from sweatshirts, satellites, motorcyclists, Stop and Go signs that make the newest works halfway stations between reality and the eclipse of the subconscious, images that stay open between life and feeling and are transfused by both. He has created a private, very modern Hades in which the symbols are given meaning by fixations that at the same time mask that meaning. That is why his work is so unique. His moralities are without a moral; heavily literary, his work resists literary explanation. His pictures are situated at that crossroads where logic and the imagination transgress each other.

March 1964
The New York Times

William Wiley

SOMETIMES an exhibition cuts away all the convenient points of reference that help you get things into perspective. These are the ones that really make you work hard; and coping with William Wiley's show at Staempfli's is a kind of hard labor. Right away, let me offer a conclusion and then arrive at it: Wiley is a disturbingly brilliant artist, going somewhere by means as convoluted as an intestinal tract, which is what some of his paintings remind you of.

His Surrealism—to grab an easy label—provokes a psychological curiosity immediately frustrated, since he gives you enough to speculate on, but not enough to form conclusions. Everything remains open, alienated, keeping you mentally off balance. (This effect was also produced recently by two shows at the Nordness Gallery, those of David Oxtoby and John Lennard, both of whom seem to have evolved a laconic post-Pop style by crossing Pop with Surrealism—a difficult hybrid to deal with.)

Wiley, now twenty-seven, is a young prodigy. I saw a show of his in San Francisco in 1961 that was a breathtaking display of muscle, and ever since have been waiting for him to arrive here. Last December he did what looks (from the photographs) like a pungent decor and costumes for Jarry's *Ubu Roi*.

His theme seems to be a neurological exploration of mind-body relationships through circuits and symbols charged with obsession, a sort of Surrealist cybernetics. The pyramid (in boxes, paintings, drawings) dominates his work, invaded by tubers with hairy ends, and frequently bearing bilobed attachments—like an image of conjoint ego and id. This motif appears and disappears throughout his work, surrounded by interrupted lines stammering along, by islands that encyst themselves, by repetitive linear annotations that have some of the virtuosity of Mary Bauermeister's magic writing. By juggling all of these in an odd dimension created by repetition and interruption, he achieves an effect like that of teasing out strategic brain cells with a series of needles, constantly jerking us into reflex thought.

The large paintings are generally not successful, muffling instead of monumentalizing small interior insights. The best of them, "Columbus Rerouted No. 3," uses a stunning variety of technical means to sustain a variety of forms and colors in an alienated limbo where the processes of thought are symbolically transposed into the processes that make up outside events. Wiley is an odd force.

March 1964
The New York Times

Cool and Violent: Goodyear and Appel

TRADITIONALISTS will detest John Goodyear's show at the Amel Gallery. Members of newly installed establishments will find it mechanical and meaningless. It is, in fact, a display of invention and virtuosity within strict disciplines, a show in which intelligence manipulates feeling with the exact and removed precision of those handling devices for shielded radioactive material.

Superficially, his constructions are easy enough to describe. A basic pattern hangs on the wall—grids, concentric parabolas, etc. Hanging in front of it, suspended from the ceiling, are from one to four lattices, painted in further patterns. From the front you can look through the interstices of space sectioned rather like an egg crate. Then you set the hanging screens moving to and fro, producing optical waves and shivers as color, design, and movement mesh and unmesh. At times it looks a bit like Mondrian's "Broadway Boogie-Woogie" separated out into planes and set in motion. The effects vary from the excessively simple to the marvelously complex.

A great deal of the fascination lies in the disparity between the obvious logic of the constructions, when you analyze them, and their contradiction of that logic when you set them in motion. Then they engage the eye in a dialogue in which both eye and object are constantly changing—setting in motion a series of relativities so interdependent that they establish a new union between object and eye. The observer, forced to participate, is pushed into a charted sea of relationships, continually breaking and reforming.

Here, of course, one is right in the middle of the revolution in art taking place all around us now.

The best of these constructions are so intriguing that one wonders what it would be like if they were enlarged to environmental size, so that one could walk through them, physically becoming part of a kaleidoscopic play of optical illusions, discovering one's own Marienbad. Since the new developments in art are constantly aspiring to the environment, art seems to be holding out promise of a remarriage with architecture.

Those who accuse the new art of being emotionless or without content should discover in Goodyear's show that the content is *in* the relationships, the sequential dissonances, the optical shocks, harmonics and rhythms that may make his—and others'—work revive the terminology of the obsolete art-as-music school of criticism. His is a giving and rewarding activity that will inevitably become art as our definition of "art" expands to include it. For those who need the security of a foothold in the "real" world, his astigmatic shivers and shock waves have many parallels in everyday experience—as when one plays with a Venetian blind or watches a railing segment a landscape as one drives by. With this show Goodyear becomes one of the leaders of the new school of "Optical" Abstraction—a mode of art he discovered for himself in isolation in Michigan in 1959.

The new "Optical" art, forfeiting overt emotion for systems of relationships that at one extreme deny emotion, and at the other refine it, forces one to turn a purged eye on Expressionism. The critical divining rod that distinguishes genuine emotion from forced or spurious sentimentalism has received a sort of overhaul.

Karel Appel's work suffers perhaps more than it should after one looks at Goodyear's fastidious union of means and end. With Appel means and end are always tearing apart, like a balloon leaving its basket behind.

This wouldn't be worth going into if Appel hadn't made major contributions up to the late fifties. Since then he has committed himself so totally to a Dionysian violence that it has become a noose strangling his work. At Stephen Hahn's, he has a churned-out series of nudes that, apart from a few good gouaches, look like fashion models twisting and turning in a maelstrom of meaningless insult. One has only to compare them to de Kooning's majestic "Women" to watch Appel's wither.

And at Martha Jackson's, Appel has reduced a positive new trend in painting (assimilation of real objects) to mere farcical play by sticking the contents of a toy shop on painted figures to make obvious puns. Some of his wooden pieces are better.

But the problem for Appel is how to return from the cul-de-sac in which he has bottled himself. His attempts to get out look like the energy of desperation. Appel needs to give his works a long, cold appraisal. Otherwise his art will surely trickle away to phantom agonies, ghost-painting his former successes, fooled by those critics and museum directors who haven't got the heart to tell him it's all gone wrong.

April 1964
The New York Times

Bruce Conner and His Films

Since art has turned itself inside out—from the self to the environment, from total abstraction to the object—there have naturally been changes in the way artists function. Instead of the artist as pure artist, his horizon physically limited by the four sides of a canvas and his eye turned inward on the clash of self-renewing forces, we are apparently getting a different kind of animal—the all-arounder who can perform within the category of what we think of as "art," and outside it, in other areas, when he so feels.

In recent years we have had the artist as a sort of pretheatrical impresario (Happenings), as performer (notably Robert Morris and Robert Rauschenberg), and more recently as movie-maker—including Andy Warhol and today's example, Bruce Conner. The artist as movie-maker is an old story—Man Ray, Cocteau, and Dali produced the classics—but there's a difference now, in much the same way that neo-Dada turned out not to be Dada at all, but Pop—although some persist in not seeing the difference.

Thus one can look at Bruce Conner's new exhibition at the Alan Gallery and at his two films, *A Movie* (1958) and *Cosmic Ray* (1962)—twelve and four minutes long respectively—as expressions of the same attitude and fundamentally the same technique applied to different mediums. At the moment assemblage as a technique is permeating all the arts with extraordinary vigor.

Conner's assemblages have curtained off a special horror corner in art in recent years. Deeply melodramatic, they provoke hostility by their careful offensiveness. There is a love of ugliness presented with a *fin-de-siècle* sense of connoisseurship—vulgarity and bad taste (or what we associate with them) consciously invited in and preserved in an environment where they retain enough to shock but not to disrupt. Take one piece: a scorched, melted head with a few teeth biting out from it; nearby a bride from a wedding cake whose groom is laid out under glass next to her. It's called "November 22nd, 1963."

It is Grand Guignol with a difference. Most of his pieces find the same sore spot and rub: flowers take on the paralysis of graveyard bouquets; girlie photos make the viewer feel like a corpse remembering former pleasures; lace associates directly with arsenic; flickering votive lamps desecrate instead of sanctify. The detritus and debris of old nylons, comic strips, wrappers, beads, cigarette butts, are accumulated in a sort of inspired excess that becomes a curious digestive process in which fire seems catalytic—everything burned and singed so it looks as if one puff of air would disperse the whole flimsy structure. The afterlife of these discarded things is as precarious as an assemblage of shadows.

In *A Movie* the technique is exactly the same—a montage of found materials from fact (newsreels) and fiction (old movies). Clichés and horrors make a rapid collage in which destruction and sex follow each other in images of pursuit (cowboys and Indians, all kinds of cars, engines, an elephant) and falling (parachutes, bombs, planes) until finally a diver disappears through a hole in the bottom of the sea—the ultimate exit. The entire thing is prefaced by a girl from a shady movie lazily undressing. By the time *A Movie* is over she has retroactively become an Eve or Circe or Prime Mover.

Some of the collage images are so well known (the *Hindenburg* in flames, Mussolini and Petacci hanging upside down, the Tacoma suspension bridge undulating like a piece of malignant rubber) that they send the mind pinwheeling out of the movie on a tangent while the next sequence is also demanding attention—a very new kind of split-level effect the way Conner does it.

For the film clips of reality are used as objects—not as objects prompting Surrealist associations, but as objects from real life loudly claiming attention while being forced into a relationship to contribute to the movie. The movie is split open again and again by real life hurtling through it. This is remarkably like the effect Robert Rauschenberg gets in his latest paintings.

The shorter film ties up closely with a piece called "Spiral Flesh" from the present show—an elbow-shaped jigsaw of what looks like fingers rotating to prompt serialized associations of the human form.

Cosmic Ray turns the female nude into a piece of animated protoplasm that pulses, expands, bursts like a bubble, overlaid by a measles of blips and flashes and numbers (and eventually more sinister images)—like an X-ray of a teen-ager's mind when Ray Charles sings "What Did I Do?" which he does on the accompanying sound track. It is a Pop-art masterpiece, with a sophistication of means, a control of ambiguous effects and expressive intent far removed from Surrealism. Conner clarifies the artistic usage of "reality"—objects and photographs and film clips—in a new way of coping with the environment. His films are revolutionary.

April 1964
The New York Times

Ortman and Kuriloff

GEORGE ORTMAN's unique painting-constructions—new examples of which are at the Howard Wise Gallery—are by now classics in modern American art, and never was the name "classic" more apt. For his work is assembled from a superstructure of geometry that is eventually taken down—so that the common heraldry guiding our everyday lives plays calmly (and absurdly) on our conditioned reflexes: arrows, stars, crosses, circles, hearts, clubs, diamonds. They are so fixed into the constructions that they assume a meaning as elusive as their symbolism is obvious.

Common symbols (or rather signs) in an uncommon situation, they play a sort of concertina of extremes: everyday and esoteric, distant and immediate, ancient and modern, universal and specific. Ortman handles them with a slow and slightly baffled sense of their immense age and their immense vitality. This gravity, augmented by pure symbolic color, makes him a symbolic classicist, as, for instance, Piero was, and like Piero, one with a deep interest in the structural basis of composition.

Here one discovers that Ortman, a most conscientious investigator of what he is doing, is engaged in a geometer's search for the sources of his symbols. In his last show he attempted to relate the symbols to the human figure, ending up with unconvincing relationships but with a source of new motifs. Currently he is anatomizing the composition and psychological motivations of old masters, notably Botticelli's "Primavera" and Gauguin's "Where do we come from . . . ?," discovering the harmonics of the Botticelli and the intuitive scheme of the Gauguin.

These discoveries, and the reconstructed, anatomized paintings which are his laboratory of exploration, are not in themselves important—except to Ortman. For by reducing the old masters to a sort of computer-style symbolic logic he has found a source of endless renewal for his symbols and compositions. The centerpiece of the "Primavera" becomes a geometer's ideal—a majestic yellow arrow defined by interrupted circles and outer darkness, a new departure in his art and one of the best things he has done. It is a marvelously original example of art feeding on art and of thoroughly genuine art springing triumphantly from doubtful premises.

This is reminiscent of the Yeatsian practice of using a framework of ideas, themselves questionable, as a basis for creations which, when finished, can survive completely without these ideas, a practice that enables the artist to create hard realities from illusions by pretending the illusions are true—a very modern relationship between means and end.

Ortman's symbols are also frequently constructed separately on small canvases inlaid into the larger ones, the lips and edges of these inlays tilted slightly to emphasize the constructed aspect. Here one comes to the fundamental effect of his art. His symbols, deprived of function, become not symbols or signs (i.e., things standing for or referring to something else), but things. His painting-constructions become not icons but objects. Symbol and sign are stripped down to their inner identity, a sort of object-identity, and the mystery of the symbol becomes the mystery of the thing.

This is close to the reason why Aaron Kuriloff's show at the Fischbach Gallery is fascinating too. He has filled the gallery with things—everyday things, freshened and presented as if they were precious: fuseboxes, switches, electrical charts, receipts, pails, pillows. Such things as radiator pipes and ventilators disappear into walls, implying systems that do not exist. Like Ortman's, you could call these objects classical—their geometry accords with the careful specifications of an anonymous draftsman for mass production.

They are not just simple ready-mades. They are carefully mounted and displayed with a calm unobtrusiveness that is underplayed and skillful. In an exact reversal of what Ortman has done, Kuriloff has made symbols out of things. His objects are forced to stand for themselves, to re-present themselves, and in doing so to become symbols of the environment, their muteness eloquent with their displacement.

Both of these shows, one turning symbols into objects, the other objects into symbols, make a new crossroads where the traffic is getting heavier—a crossroads at which Jasper Johns originally planted his painted flags, breaking our reflex responses to the most loaded of symbols. Ortman and Kuriloff show that if art is transformation the transformation can be both ways: a phantom battle of symbols can become a solid dialogue of things; and common things can symbolize enigmas that they habitually cancel.

May 1964
The New York Times

Whitney Sculpture: Possible Futures

THRUSTING, probing, undulating and kinking through space, the pieces in the Whitney Museum's superb biennial of American sculpture make up one of the most exciting and exploratory sculpture shows in years. The aggression and attack on the third dimension constitutes the main excitement—and shock. For shock, now that everything is totally accepted by the public, has to be *learned*. It is, for the connoisseur of the new, an aesthetic reconstruction in which he must know the norm from which many of these works depart.

For these sculptures again and again break all the rules of sculpture—and the critical point is whether they create new ones, or, caught in the drag of take-off, fail to make the air safely. The word by which many of them would have been judged previously is "arbitrary," a condemnation meaning "fixed or arrived at through will or caprice, decisive but unreasoned." But now the arbitrary act of will has become the thrust of intuition, and the caprice the logic of a new vocabulary of form—and space.

The new form has been around for quite a while (it was seen sporadically in the Jewish Museum's recent "Six Sculptors"), but this is the first time one sees such a wide compendium of arbitrary forms key into the same word—"process"—made entirely logical artistically in the context of new goals, new definitions of the sculptural activity. George Sugarman is now a long-time pioneer, his polychromed wood sprouting by lumps, squiggles, pleats, undulations, and changing color and direction like a complex funicular system. David Weinrib's suspended (from an artificial ceiling) three plastic forms brilliantly confirm his wayward direction of the past few years, marrying conflicting oblongs, wedges, funnels, and color in a daring spatial continuum; John Clague's domino clutter of aseptically defined woods, called "Overture in Black and White," arches across a semicircle like a modern dancer, searching out the space within the general movement with delicate tilts, swings, oval grinds.

The sense of formal and unlimited progression can be applied to an astonishing number of those works, including those that seemingly limit the disorder of growth by placing the action in rectangular skeletons—David Gray's intestinal tangle of lead pipes, and, most surprisingly, Herbert Ferber's major success in making his welded hieroglyphics take on a new tension in their delimiting cage.

The lesson is obvious. Abstract Expressionism is carrying through into sculpture not the particulars of motif, chance, accident, but the fundamental idea of which these are merely aspects—the sense of continuation, progression, unstoppable process. A sculpture is no longer an object packaging its quota of space—but a break into something without beginning or end, which could conceivably progress environmentally on and on and on. The decision the new sculptor has to make is where he breaks in and out, calls stop or start, defining whole new parallel streams of activity—so that going from sculptor to sculptor in this show is like tuning in on a crowded shortwave band from, say, Robert Howard's crablike landscape to David Von Schlegell's beautifully engineered—and empty—curve. The old idea of a sculpture as a closed system has (in most of these works) given way to systems of alternatives in which choice opens as many possibilities as it closes.

But this is only part—though the most part—of the Whitney's dazzling spectrum of possibilities. Both kinetic and light sculpture are there, if not in full strength. Len Lye sets a steel rod pirouetting and whipping around into a solid band, and George Rickey has harvested a slow system of nodding aluminum spicules. Pop and post-Pop sculpture is infrequent (Claes Oldenburg's huge light switch made of flabby fabric, Elias Friedensohn's telephonic interpretation of Pyramus and Thisbe). Object sculpture is more or less unrecognized as a trend.

In the sparsely populated human-figure area, Frank Gallo seems a possible comer, with his nubile girl, waxily nude in polyester resin and fiberglass, melting despondently into a sling chair—an old sentiment finding tentative new form.

Among the new and moderately new arrivals:

John Anderson (thirty-eight), a tall young man who carpenters huge agricultural-looking clubs and boxing gloves from mesquite wood, counterweighs them with an anchoring bole and ends up with clumsy space probes caught between a puzzling vision of farmyard obsolescence and roughly antennaed robots. A title helps: "Big Sam's Bodyguard"—Big Sam being a huge logger Anderson worked with in a lumber camp.

Robert Rohm (thirty), who teaches at Pratt Institute, simply makes a box from the side of which an abstract arm emerges, bends its elbow, ending up in scroll-like twists and potato bulges carved from laminated wood. They key is the contrast—as with so many pieces in this show—between the box and free form, the logic of geometry and the organic arbitrary growth.

Sondra Beal (twenty-eight), whose high-relief sculpture in arbitrary wooden segments, cosmeticized by color, jumps into a profitable half-ground between painting and sculpture, again showing the more direct influence of the Abstract Expressionist generation.

A whole new generation has moved into prominence with this Whitney show (although one of the best of them, Mark di Suvero, is not represented). Its brilliant opening up of possibilities—of movement, of color, of form, of the entire sculptural vocabulary *plus* a mature ability to capitalize on these possibilities—may make this show, looking back at it from any one of many possible futures, a landmark in American sculpture.

January 1965
Newsweek

Pop Plumbing in New York

THE MOST SURPRISING thing about "Erotic Art '66," the big sexual Pop congress at the Janis Gallery, originated by Carroll Janis, is that it is not Erotic Art '65 or '64 or '63. It was in 1963 that the efflorescence of such work occurred, coinciding with the return of "subject matter" and the beginning of Pop, which, for a hectic season, vigorously deflowered abstract art and littered the galleries with large and bland banalities. In January 1964, the Pace Gallery held a sort of wave-of-the-erotic-future exhibition called, with typical Pop put-on, "The First International Girlie Show." Of course there never was a second. Since then there have been intermittent spasms, notably an exhibition at the Van Bovercamp Gallery in 1964 which, as far as I can remember, played around daringly enough with sexual apparatus, got some publicity, and ended up with businessmen queueing up during the lunch hour.

Now good fun and inventive scatology have given way, in "Erotic Art '66," to a much less urgent and, by and large, less genital approach. In ensemble—with the exception of the films which are shown in the center gallery—the work plays down the curiosities of urogenital plumbing and the rather trying delights of artists redis-covering the clichés of sexual congress. Sex is no longer an obstruc-tion to arriving at a good piece of art; and the desire to shock, the obverse of bourgeois puritanism, is sensibly obsolete. This is perhaps due to two factors. First, the gallery has simply documented the contemporary updating of a traditional subject. It is easy to overlook that such updatings haven't had serious gallery exposure before, and the very fact that this exhibition *exists* can lead to appropriate meditations. Second, I suspect that the art allows one to maintain a certain connoisseur's distance from its subject matter for a very good reason. Sex has become rather unimportant—indeed, after looking into current films and fiction it seems the one human act most casually divorced from love. Thus it is absorbed into the rest of life and handled with the same unsurprised air as any other routine subject. Sex now is simply a way people like each other. Drugs and civil rights are more "exciting" in the sense that sex used to be exciting, *i.e.*, illicit or noble.

Again there is an opportunity here to dwell on changing mores. Sexual rhetoric, like any other kind of rhetoric, has become a debased convention and the prevailing style in this show, Pop, is perfectly adapted to cooling off a once-hot subject. Indeed Pop attitudes in general are such that the exhibition may be concentrat-ing on the wrong end. For we have become an oral culture, and sexual awareness has migrated or regressed to the primary erogenous zone. Here there are tempting Freudian possibilities, all the more so since the predominant art now is militantly anti-Freudian. They can perhaps be summarized by saying that as a culture we certainly can go—as in "go-go"—but there is increasing doubt as to whether we can come. I have heard Pop art accused of cultivating this flossy impotence.

Thus this exhibition hardly raises the question of pornography, though recent United States Supreme Court decisions, especially that on Ralph Ginzburg, editor of *Eros*, have made censorship of art and literature once again a live issue in America. For instance, the catalogue (which is sent through the mails) reproduces only the upper half of Rotella's "*Operation Sade*" (oil and photography on canvas) and labels it "detail." The missing half shows an introitus surrounded by a small chain which a hand lifts upward. I assume the reason for this is a heightened sense of discretion prompted by the Supreme Court's controversial ruling. If such is the case, it only illustrates the mischief that such censorship can create by introducing a wary self-censorship destructive of full artistic expression—and in this case makes nonsense of the catalogue photograph. One can agree with the strongest dissent, by Justice Potter Stewart, in the Ralph Ginzburg case, that "Censorship reflects a society's lack of confidence in itself. It is a hallmark of an authoritarian regime . . . the Constitution protects coarse expression as well as refined, and vulgarity no less than elegance. . . . In the free society to which our Constitution has committed us, it is easy for each to choose for himself."

The artists' choice in the Janis exhibition helps close the gap between visual art and the other arts with regard to erotic sophistication—one of the areas in which visual art has been behind its time. The detached irony, the oblique and referential humor of such novelists as, say, Irvin Faust, J. P. Donleavy or Bruce Jay Friedman, has been missing in art until recently. Similarly, films— e.g., Varda's *Le Bonheur*, Godard's *The Married Woman*—have been more advanced in either dealing with sex as a biological curiosity or in absorbing sexual matters into wider human dilemmas and thus letting the full spectrum of expressive means work within this area—an area usually walled off with Anglo-Saxon guilt, pushing the treatment of sex down to the panties, bra and high-heels area of what Jack Kerouac referred to as the "Forty-Second Street jerkoff image." The artists in the Janis show—with the exception of the artist-film-makers Warhol and Watts, whose films play with titillation or make a Dada charade of apertures and pseudo-organs—make sophisticated and casual breeches into the subject so that it is invaded by the dandyism of Pop connoisseurship. (One should mention here Robert Whitman's "Shower" (1964), in which a nude is projected against the *inner* side of a shower curtain, accompanied by the recorded drumming of a shower spray. Whitman is the best of the newer artist-performer-film-makers. The realism is uncanny, and it would be simply cinematic *trompe-l'oeil* were it not for the invited qualifying realization that there is simply no one there.) This mobile ease has been notably missing from twentieth-century erotic art, which has tended to fix itself on guilt images (e.g., Rouault's whores, Schiele's starved Viennese mods) or circled around the basic theme of the copulating couple. This latter usually runs from joyous express-train collisions (e.g., Picasso's well-known etching) to innumerable blurred discretions in which brute fact is mitigated by "poetry." The closest this show comes to the latter is Marisol's bird's-eye view of severely edited fragments of a copulating couple; boxed and transilluminated, it is altogether a curious and delicate skiagram.

It is interesting to note that these modes are connected with a certain type of criticism framed by some well-worn "humanistic" attitudes and mental "sets" (i.e., expectations which delimit perception). Such criticism perceives the sexual act in terms of a self-conscious high-mindedness, its phrases run to "the mystery of human union and generation." This kind of "set criticism" is less obsolete than it should be. One wonders what such criticism would come up with if shown only the faces of some of the copulating pairs in Indian miniatures and "set" to perceive them as picking flowers. (Indeed, one of the most delightful aspects of such Indian art is the charming insouciance displayed on the faces of persons whose bodies are so cunningly interpenetrated.)

The matter of mental "set" is at the core of the trouble such exhibitions as this occasionally encounter. From previous observation, I expect some people visiting this show will see pornography even in the wall fixtures. When confronted with a work they consider dubious, I notice that they fix on an element and mentally augment it until it seems to them horrifyingly pornographic. And when asked to point out what is objectionable, they go, like an archer, to what they consider the heart of the matter—totally ignoring the rest of the work.

I think this matter of eroticism and pornography is possibly settled by a simple aesthetic rule of thumb. Pornography is a very applied art, aimed at getting down to the thalamus as quickly as possible. Thus it uses the most immediately recognizable visual conventions (of which photography is one). These are usually of a debased naturalism which the pornographee doesn't even realize *is* a convention. The more efficiently pornography functions, the more it uses the artistically debased conventions of its time, all aimed at cutting out *how* the image is transferred. It is immediate, nonsymbolic, easy to read, and in a hurry. Genuine erotic art is generally more difficult to read, cool, not in a hurry. Artistic value militates against pornographic bias. In other words, eroticism in art, even in such a brute as Courbet, turns out to be a connoisseur's language, like any other high art—just as Pop, the language of most of this exhibition, has turned out to be high art too, via the low road. Perhaps one can focus all this with what would make a telling absurdist vignette: put a bushman, who can't read a photograph, to watching a randy teen-ager with his *Playboy* center spread.

There are two other major points that this exhibition brings out, and helps in its way to elucidate. One can only touch on them here. We are constantly being told (and with good reason) that we are in the middle of a "sexual revolution." As A. H. Maslow writes, "Relations *between* the sexes are very largely determined by the relationship between masculinity and femininity *within* each person, male or female." The area of neutralization and sexual blurring within *and* between individuals is now established enough to be copy for women's magazines. This arrival of an apparent "new" neuter on the scene is explicable, I think, in two ways: (1) The definitions of masculine and feminine roles are being radically altered by a new generation whose idea of these roles doesn't fit in with those of their parents, and which are, of course, formed completely outside their elders' lingering Victorian conception of guilt. Essentially this is progressive, though to some it may appear bizarre in habits, attitudes, and dress. (2) Opposite to this is genuine neutralization: the classic shell of alienation enclosing a creature whose responses are superficial but inventive, cool but curiously arresting, swinging but verging on the hysterical. This is of course where some Pop artists have been placed, and their work has done nothing to disprove it. None of the works at Janis falls easily into either of these categories, but perhaps Larry Rivers' robotized lover, providing *vis a tergo* for a bending partner, makes connections with both through a subtle humor. Jim Dine's "Green Table and Chairs" looks like the second, but in a triumph of a definite sort is actually more in the area of the first. Dine's piece is the best in the show, although his previous art has for me remained ambivalent rather than ambiguous, as if he had arrived a few years too late and really belongs to the generation of Rivers, Rauschenberg and Johns. But in this piece—two chairs and a table that say "table" and "chair" as in a child's book, the front margin of each seat being joined together via a hose which falls in redundant coils on the ground between—the ambiguity is absorbed in a unitary statement of virtually hyaline consistency. The work remains as brightly interrogative as a raised isolated eyebrow, the ironies are concealed, the dialectic not suppressed but anesthetized, as it were—which is by way of being a definition of good Pop.

The other major point to which this exhibition relates is the old chestnut of body image. But now the body image has broken down into isolated body parts. A major show remains to be done, not on the new image of man in any holistic sense, but in terms of the pigeonholing and implications of body parts. They have become a major thematic mode in art, and the spectrum of attitudes and anatomy is extremely wide. It is a genuinely international phenomenon and has a decided history in modern art, though its present impetus seems to come from advertising and the cinema. Indeed the essay on body parts during the love scene became almost obligatory in New Wave films (and no one has handled it as well as Godard). The Janis exhibition is full of such objectifications—Fahlstrom's movable digits in his picture of "Sylvie," the French singer; Allen Jones's falling "Great Divide"; Tom Wesselmann's huge pushbutton breast arching into the wide blue yonder; Watts's anatomical jigsaw; Stevenson's artichoke-like core isolated between two huge and tender fingers. In general the parts are private, their function plumbing. But the art is such that the private parts are publicly innocuous, the plumbing not uncharming.

November 1966
Art and Artists

The Armory Show

THE MAJOR scandale, triumph, vision, or nightmare of the season were the events—planned and unplanned—that took place from October 13 to 23 at the 25th Street Armory on Lexington Avenue. It is a measure of the events' aesthetic diversity and of the audiences' multiple expectations that it was all these things at more or less the same time. Called 9 Evenings: Theater and Engineering, it ended up by disproving its own title, for it was neither theater nor, in the last analysis, engineering, that was the essential of the occasion. Nor, as it happened, was the liaison between them consummated with any great degree of efficiency. Yet the impact of the affair has been enormous, and its afterlife, in film and still photos, begins to qualify and change what actually took place. These records tend to be more impressively imaginative than the events themselves; the historical audience, seeing textbook photos, will regret they were not there. The actual audience often regretted that they were.

What really happened at the Armory—the Armory, site of the 1913 Armory Show that force-fed the American public on modern art—was that a crisscross of traditions, disciplines, time streams, and audiences got together in a huge, short-circuited tangle. Depending on which strand you get hold of and follow, you can end up with entirely different conclusions.

It is a tangle worth sorting out, since "Evenings" received, on the whole, an appalling press—based mainly on the justifiable irritation of interminable delays, technical failures of the most basic sort, and long, dead spaces between, and sometimes in the middle of, pieces. Yet, as such irritations fade away, one is left with startlingly persistent residual images, and strong hints of an alternative theater that has been lagging in its post-Happenings penumbra between art and theater, there tending to cultivate its own clichés.

The whole thing was, I understand, planned to happen 4,000 miles away—in Stockholm, at a Festival of Art and Technology to which Rauschenberg, Fahlstrom, Oldenburg, Dine, among others, were invited. Dine and Oldenburg, already in Europe, were simply to have gone to Stockholm. But a disagreement on the exact relationship of technicians to the artists (prophetic friction!) led to the cancellation of plans. So the group, including Yvonne Rainier, Alex and Deborah Hay, Steve Paxton and Lucinda Childs, minus Oldenburg and Dine, and augmented by John Cage and David Tudor, went ahead—first of all flushing sponsors from the rich New York coverts, then searching for a space in which to work.

The sponsors came through with close to $90,000—a large sum for an artistic venture, but in theatrical terms a small piece of bread in New York, "just about enough," as someone remarked, "to get your first act on." The space turned out to be the Armory, home of the "Fighting 69th" (appropriately enough, a large-screen James Cagney, who played in that movie, appeared in Yvonne Rainier's piece).

The space was frightening to anyone except a regiment—a vertically sliced barrel arching over like a gigantic Nissen hut, from the top of which cables drooped and hung where they had been set by riggers a hundred feet up in the twilight. (Paxton's 100-foot vertical tube of inflated plastic was the "Evenings'" most impressive formal unit.) The audience was lined up in three bleachers blocks on one side of the floor. Dwarfed by a vertical cliff of air, the space needed extremely sophisticated lighting to establish some kind of control over it. This was provided. Lighting was one of the "Evenings'" few technical successes. But the space raised major problems of focus and diffusion—gymnasium rather than stage management. Generally it was used as a vast table, with screens set up in rows facing the audience. The tidiest and neatest use of the space was Deborah Hay's "Solo," in which stripped-down men and women moved and expanded in a white evenly lit space, walking, pairing, sometimes making cramped, amoeboid movements—as if their limbs had been blunted—on floats controlled by nine people set up against the distant wall. It was one of the few pieces that did exactly what it set out to do.

But really, one should begin with the audience, 1,500 each night. It included, on opening night, virtually everyone with a "New York Scene" label attached. Had the roof fallen, there would have been no more American art. The audience remained one of the "Evenings'" main phenomena. It appeared to be composed of what Harold Rosenberg calls the "avant-garde audience," plus the mod-discothèque lot, plus the new philistines who have been sold on art by Life magazine. The latter responded with applause ironically aimed at whatever obviously didn't work, or finally did work; the mod group seemed more interested in themselves than in the events; and the avant-gardists were disappointed because they weren't really confronted with anything "new." (After a decade of avant-gardism, the audience in New York is out in front of the artists, who more and more suspect the value of the "new.") Lastly, the audience included a number of irate engineers who felt—with reason—that their profession had been let down. All the above were unfairly set with high expectations by publicity that promised technological miracles of the "see-the-man-walk-on-water" variety. The emphasis was wrongly placed on technological aids rather than on the clarification of a relatively new art form.

One of the premises of this kind of post-Happenings activity is audience involvement. The Armory was set up so that this proved virtually impossible. The only one who solved this problem was John Cage. His piece—a typical one—created a solid continuum of noise which appeared chaotic until *instinctively* one began to separate out different streams, repetitions, identifications—all forcing multiple experiences with the real-life fright removed. It blared, on its first night at a passively frozen audience. The second night ("Were you there the first night or the second night?" became one of the "Evenings'" primary questions; each of the pieces was repeated once) Cage seeded the audience with people who left the bleachers during the performance and walked around the electronic clutter frantically serviced by technicians whose shadows were thrown on a white screen—a typically Cagean palimpsest gathering in the evening's activity. The audience followed in dribbles and then in one great flood, ending up clustering and shifting on the floor. This was undoubtedly a major success.

But the focus of the "Evenings"—and the standard by which they were judged—was a wrong one. Technology was played up far too much, a residue of the machine adulation that is no longer an issue. The artists as well as the technicians have to take some of the blame for its failures—although anyone acquainted with the intractable and treacherous nature of machines can fully sympathize.

Here we must get back to why the series was canceled in Stockholm. The Swedes, as I understand it, wanted the artists to relay their technical problems to the engineers, who would simply solve them. But the New York group wanted to work *with* the technicians—follow their thinking, involve them in the artist's way of thinking. This makes great demands on patience, mutual understanding, and above all, time. Ideally it would acquaint the artists with their new materials, since art often arises out of the nature of materials themselves.

This democratic idea is especially typical of Rauschenberg's equal respect for all materials, which in this case included people. It was followed with the cooperating Bell Telephone engineers. But more practical and immediate results might have been forthcoming by treating the technicians as problem-solving animals, and allowing them no more existence than that. The making of art, especially in group situations, is not a very democratic process—as some European groups have made clear. Yet it is to the credit of the "Evenings" that they pioneered a one-to-one artist-technician relationship. For example, program notes went: "Physical Things by: Steve Paxton—Performance Engineer: Dick Wolff." This tandem idea may be the right one in the long run. But it needs years to bear fruit, not months. Seen in this perspective the "Evenings" were an extraordinary success.

A grave impediment to this marriage of art and technology was the climate of ideas in which most of the artists matured. Abstract Expressionist ideas of process achieve their most tenacious survival in this activity situated between the canvas and the theater. One wing of pre-Pop and Pop (especially Oldenburg and Dine) inherits its timely sense of continuous engagement with the materials of art. This is in contradistinction to the commercially derived wing of Pop. For instance, Warhol's essay into sight and sound environment—his "Exploding Plastic Inevitable"—has a smooth professionalism the "Evenings" lacked.

It must have been agonizing for the engineers to come to any sort of terms with that built-in sense of indeterminacy and process. This was the gulf that yawned widest at the Armory. Either the engineers have to provide a superflexibility of means or the artists have to modify their ideas on freedom and chance to meet the technical limitations of the fairly new medium of technology itself. The artists' ideas were nearly always imaginative and often brilliant. But part of one's frequent anguish at the Armory was watching good ideas fail.

Alex Hay's and Rauschenberg's pieces were in the purest line of development of the Happenings ideas, and thus the medium in which they worked received some clarification. The Hay involved wiring the body for muscle sound, brain waves, heartbeat, etc. (that body-parts business again), amplified while he randomly distributed a group of numbered cloth squares—which task done, he seated himself before a huge screen on which his head was projected via live TV, while two orderlies reheaped the squares in correct sequence. It would, like many of the pieces, look marvelous on film, where the sense of focus would provide the "missing" psychological interest. But this missing interest, this lack of tension, was the event's main content, and the audience, having no idea how to savor it, was restive.

Rauschenberg offered a two-part piece with an extraordinary postscript. A game of tennis was played by a couple (Mimi Kanarek, Frank Stella) with electrified racquets (his sound a masculine *bong*, hers a feminine *bing*), each contact of ball and racquet depleting the lighting until the game haltingly broke up in semidarkness. At that point, a prerecording of the *bing-bong* sound took over, like a great bell, as an invisible crowd of five hundred assembled on the Armory floor, projected in delayed radarscope images on three screens by infrared TV. They moved, with light cues from the balcony, in some sort of loosely structured concert. It was a majestic and successful conception, finally succeeded by a sort of single-cell postscript, an animate, completely wrapped bundle carried by Rauschenberg from place to place, followed by a spotlight, while the limbless bundle sang, indestructible through it all like some Yeatsian ragamatag.

Two other major pieces were infinitely more diverse, theatrical, propagandist, literary. Robert Whitman, the newest and brightest addition to the genre, did some brilliant things in "Two Holes of Water" (particularly a slowly moving tableau elasticized by concave mirrors and projected on a large screen). Oyvind Fahlstrom put on a staggering display of inventiveness, ranging from idiot savants to ceremonial profanation of President Johnson's modeled head (which bore a large hole in its occiput). Boschian in feeling, its iconography was similarly profuse. It would require a separate article to deal with it in any efficient way.

It is hard to characterize the quality that separates these "Evenings" from the Happenings of the classic era, say, 1958 to 1963. The pressures that forced an attack on prevailing artistic conventions have been mitigated. The anti-conventions then established are now conventions themselves, with all the easy traps of avant-garde conformity: randomness, chance, simultaneity, lack of climax and resolution, dissociation of parts. They are now old-fashioned as modes. What matters is what they can be made to yield as conventions.

Emerging most strongly is the equal emphasis of parts, whether concurrent or sequential. One bit of data or one activity is as good as another, whether it is so-called reality or a reality surrogate (TV and film images). This equal weighing of experience, in which noise may be music and any visual image art, produced what one might call a time density, a time situation in which a tube of constructed activities is squeezed solid. Obviously this idea derives from Cage and Merce Cunningham, but they gave it to visual art via Rauschenberg, who allied it to some Abstract Expressionist characteristics. I feel it is the artists' experience that left its mark most strongly on the "Evenings." The ideas were mainly passed through artists' sensibilities, not through dancers'. A capacity is developing to handle the density and valency of this time structure, to perfect the smoothness of its concurrent flow, to mingle and separate its parts with more authority, to locate and dislocate the senses in a way far more subtle and artlike than does the shotgun discothèque psyche-delic scene. This time density is, in Whitman and Fahlstrom, approaching certain narrative elements that the earlier era would have rejected, making stronger connections with Surrealism and with Expressionist film. With the Hay and the Rauschenberg, the anti-literary prejudices prevail and the Happenings idea is purified and strengthened by a certain rigorous formalism, a formalism somewhat now in Rauschenberg's work. Thus the "Evenings" gave us both wings of the post-Happenings development—literary-baroque extravaganzas and nonliterary, beautifully organized con-tinuums. The technical devices at the Armory were simply to aid these processes to realize themselves. The fact that they largely failed to do so in no way lessens the importance of what was attempted.

December 1966
Art and Artists

Narcissus in Hades

THE SURFACING of Andy Warhol's underground film *The Chelsea Girls* has provoked the predictable range of responses, so predictable that they begin to assume a ritualistic character. These responses are of course totally polar, with nothing between moral outrage and uncritical enthusiasm. This yes-no dialogue of com-puterlike naïveté tends to respond to the film's milieu rather than to the film itself.

The very appearance of *Chelsea Girls* overground is itself remark-able, for it pressured its way upward from an extended showing at the Cinemathèque on West 41st Street—the center of the under-ground establishment—to a bona fide first-run house at the slightly higher than usual price of $3 per person. The movie thus made it the hard way, on its merits—all the more surprising since its author's name has become almost synonymous with making it easy in the big town.

Chelsea Girls forces one to reverse nearly every preconception about Warhol. Ostensibly a split-screen probing of the West 23rd Street Chelsea Hotel's interior, it is doubtless a major film in its ambition and execution, quite possibly the first masterpiece from a generation that has learned to handle the medium of film as casually as an artist used to handle paint long ago before painting was threatened with obsolescence. Thus the film illuminates the nature of a medium that has been totally conventionalized by the narrative Hollywood tradition, a tradition that has quickly absorbed any breaks in that convention to reinforce itself. In his way, what Warhol tries to do for the film is in the order of what Joyce did with the novel, and it is a measure of Warhol's achievement that the comparison is not laughable.

The *persona* that Warhol has hitherto presented has been that of a de-cerebrate Peter Pan, with silver shock of hair, dark glasses, and simulated babble. By means of it he has kept everything at a happily uncritical distance, expertly putting on art, criticism and the Pop scene. This has covered up a mind of remarkable intuition and no little intelligence, though one was usually left with an impression of a defensive attitude that subverted its function into a kind of connoisseurship of subversion itself. This led to some interesting dialogues between his art and attitudes to art, both formally and psychologically. He developed a remarkable aptitude for providing stimuli to polemics and dialectical warfare while standing back with the surprised innocence of a child who just happened to light a fuse. Some paintings—the repetitions of Grand Guignol material such as car crashes and the electric chair—have made violence almost chic, putting on the sado-masochistic bit while indulging it. Other images (the soup cans, Marilyn, the recent bulls' heads) have purposely depreciated into a kind of wallpaper, in their own way assassinating the idea of painting. Some of his previous films (*Empire, Sleep*) have actually pioneered the idea of the film as wallpaper.

All this shows a dazzling gift for surface, and Warhol has, with great sophistication, cultivated a sort of brilliant infantile tropism for glitter. His gifts have also been lavished on another kind of surface, his *persona* and its relation to the world. This, of course, is a kind of narcissism turned into style of life, the now-familiar sixties dandy as mod swinger. Translated into cinema, the camera lens becomes the eye of this surrogate self, and Warhol has turned it on the stock characters of the underworld—homosexuals, lesbians, drug addicts, masochists, sadists, *et al*. But with a difference. There is a complete absence of put-on, and in meeting the full implications of his own point of view, Warhol avoids the stylish cop-out he has turned into an art form of a sort. This has led to an extraordinary union of his gift for the obvious and a sort of calm, hysterical profundity. It manifests itself in a concurrence of movement and stasis, triviality and impotence, chic and *Angst*, surface and depth. It is a strange near-amalgam, somewhat as if *Last Exit to Brooklyn* had been crossed with *Grand Hotel*. The whole ambience tends, through a very carefully handled effect of boredom, to dissociate mind and body, and thus to become metaphysical. Warhol's world is as de-realizing as William Burroughs' and its surface is as narcotic and beautiful. The absence of narrative direction, the purposeless to-and-fro movement within which action merely emphasizes paralysis, and the random spasms of sensuality are common to both. Time in both Burroughs and Warhol is a matter of continuums packed with material, progressing nowhere, just as the action occurs in, essentially, noplace. It is as if Warhol had turned himself loose as a kind of Narcissus in Hades.

The action, such as it is, is made up for the most part of the troughs between crises—deviates dallying, bitches bitching, addicts mainlining, somnambulistic wanderings in which characters cross from room to room (screen to screen), set pieces, improvisations, and, of course, people doing—*nothing*; although nothing, like boredom, depending on the frame of reference, becomes a productive entity. The episodes, concurrently staggered by means of the two projectors, bring on a set of characters that make up an underground Who's Who. Surprisingly, nearly every character has density and presence, in itself a tribute to the way in which Warhol has developed not actors, but people who are able to slide in and out of a way of forgetting about the camera and returning to a more or less oblique awareness of it, at the same time processing their own lives, that is, to put it crudely, being themselves—even when they improvise another role.

There are some remarkable tours de force, including an interminable maternal harangue, a monumental homosexual tantrum (real, not acted—and the way that Warhol handles this unexpected bonanza, which would totally disrupt a conventional film, is marvelous: the camera sweeps around in calm orbits over the momentarily deserted set, until the missing character ends his offstage battle and returns), and a somnambulistic soliloquy of the kind that experimental film (and even Jean-Luc Godard) has constantly failed to put across. Bathed in washes of indigo and mauve, a wide-eyed, stripteasing character, observed from the left-hand screen by a Caravaggesque group, puts himself through an extraordinary kind of amoeboid regression, all the time dead-panning a soliloquy that is probably the closest Warhol will ever come to a testament—his attitudes to pleasure, the world, his handling of the world's attitudes to him. It is a superb set piece, a sort of Molly Bloom in drag, and it is the clearest point of entry into the existential vacuum Warhol has so brilliantly voyeured.

With Chelsea Girls Warhol perfects the double image that he has tested in previous films as a viable mode of handling long durations (Chelsea Girls is three and a half hours long) without a narrative thread. One image tends to take precedence, the other underpins it, taking in any of the viewer's inattention or psychological spillover. He has also perfected some techniques that appear random but are in fact carefully effective. If one follows the idea of the camera lens as the semidetached eye of Warhol's *persona*, it becomes an instrument sensitive to the random impulses that the eye itself picks up, zooming in and out on whatever catches its attention—irrelevant details of clothing and environment, body parts, crotches; it wanders, overexposes, blurs, holds glassily still. This whole process, which starts as a sort of commentary against the subject matter, ends up absolutely fused with it. The camera seems to be finally projecting Warhol's underworld as well as observing it. Only an eye—but what an eye.

February 1967
Art and Artists

PART TWO

PATRONS
AND MUSEUMS

Death of a Gallery

ALTHOUGH one could hardly call it a cradle of genius, the Tanager Gallery, a small single room with a large shop window at 90 East Tenth Street, rocked some highly respectable talents. Its passing—it is scheduled to close in summer 1962—is a cause for regret, for the Tanager must have a definite footnote in any social history of New York.

For the past ten years, with costs rising in Greenwich Village, the cry to the young artist has been, "Go East, young man." The Tanager blazed the trail eastward, and was the first gallery in an area known more for its human flotsam than for the *objet trouvé*. For many artists it was their social club, their communications center, their parish hall. In short, it served a community, especially in the early days. A gallery can ask no higher purpose.

The Tanager began when five persons living on the East Side without benefit of gallery got together and decided to start one. They were Angelo Ippolito, Charles Cajori, Bill King, Lois Dodd and Fred Mitchell. In the spring of 1952 they found a place (now torn down) on Third Avenue at East Fourth Street. One of the windows of the gallery *manqué* was painted a bright orange, as storeroom windows sometimes are. This fascinated the painters. After they had got a few bad attempts at christening, such as "The Orange Blot," out of their systems, someone (obviously a symbolist) said, "Why not call it the Tanager? A tanager is red." A tanager, for all of us who don't know, is "any of numerous American oscine birds constituting the family Thraupidae."

A year later, in the spring of 1953, another artist, Perle Fine, sent word that a large room in front of her studio on Tenth Street was going for less than what they were paying. They immediately moved. They took the name, the Tanager Gallery, with them; this title, according to the present director, Enid Furlonger, still gives trouble to non-ornithologists, who come looking for the "Teenager" Gallery. From 1954 on, the other galleries started opening—the Marsh Gallery, the Area, the Camino, the Carmel. The rather dilapidated street was christened by one wag as "The Slopes of Parnassus."

A new gallery needs two things to survive: art and money. The latter preferably accrues from the former. Artists showing at the Tanager paid for their own catalogues, were not charged any gallery fee and initially paid only 25 per cent commission on sales to the co-op. This remarkable innovation in commissions was subsequently raised by economic necessity to the standard 33 per cent. Sales were never startling, however, and it was years before the public began to come. But an exhibiting artist was always assured an audience of fellow artists—a sobering thought.

Eventually Tenth Street became famous. Discriminating tourists learned that Tenth Street was "the real thing." It certainly had character. Bums exposed by the tearing down of the Third Avenue El, blinking in the unaccustomed daylight, drifted in and out of Tenth Street, and sometimes you had to step over them to get into a gallery. The stoops were littered with newspaper-wrapped wine bottles which the bums had emptied and replaced with some of their bodily fluids. During the height of the street's fame, all the galleries cooperated on a Christmas show, all opening the same day and sharing a common catalogue. Such cooperation brought a columnist hot-footing down from the Daily Worker happily suspecting signs of imminent socialism. "He was," says Lois Dodd, "disappointed. He wasn't much interested in the art."

In the last few years, it is generally admitted, the character of the area (and of the art) has begun to change. Many of the fine artists graduated uptown to the warm embrace of the dealer and the carpeted gallery. The avant-garde split into splinter groups with as many fine distinctions, social and otherwise, as at a vicar's tea party in an English village. The Tanager, which has always had a sense of its own short history, and is currently showing work done before 1952 by artists later associated with the gallery, will close in June.

Why is it closing? No one can quite put a finger on it, or appears willing to. Economics again are a factor, although the co-op has been generously backed by a patron (the father of one of the painters, Sally Hazelet Drummond) for the last few years. Then, Tenth Street has changed. And some artists have, as mentioned, gone uptown; others have dropped out. All of them are ten years older.

Perhaps this is the real reason. The gallery served one community and one generation. Having accomplished that purpose, it is finished. A new generation can take care of itself. This is refreshing. In an age when people serve institutions, one small group of artists created an institution to serve them, and when it ceased to do so it became unnecessary. Thus the Tanager will die a natural death.

The gallery, to allow a small genuflection to sentiment, will persist impermanently and for a while in the memories of many, and in the hearts of some artists remembering days of struggle in the big town.

April 1962
The New York Times

The Museum of Primitive Art

"SCULPTURE FROM THE PACIFIC," the Museum of Primitive Art's fine summer show, came quietly—as usual—to the converted mansion on 54th Street occupied by New York's youngest museum. Fifty-fourth Street in this block is a highly aesthetic patch of

Manhattan. Across the road is the garden of New York's most spectacular social center, the Museum of Modern Art. Just up the block is the slablike front of the more introverted Whitney Museum of American Art. Going up the street, with your head turned by these two museums, you could easily miss the unobtrusive Museum of Primitive Art.

The present show is typical of the museum. The quality of the objects—ancestor figures, charms, shields, ornaments—is excellent; the catalogue is tersely informative, with just enough to satisfy the casual and provoke the curious; the display is imaginatively theatrical, with spotlights picking the objects out of a twilight that stimulates the imagination, but is not so dark that one must grope around. Particularly effective is the display of four famous pieces from the late Sir Jacob Epstein's collection, including the superb African head called "The Great Bieri," suspended in its cage like a large inverted drop and as classical in its own way as the Bartlett Aphrodite.

The museum, which opened in 1957, is unusual in a number of ways, apart from its contents. It goes about its work quietly. It tends to let the public come to it rather than to go out and get it with the Pepsodent smile and the colored brochure. It has developed its own public, and a membership of around five hundred, and has been wary of the chic popularity that would make primitive objects the trinkets of a society oversophisticated to brashness.

Its policy might be called progressive-conservative, one that combines a respect for the objects in its care with a respect for the public that wishes to find out about them. It is a thoughtful museum and has even given thought, in retrospect, to its name.

Primitive art might be defined as the art of communities that have not learned to conjugate cause and effect with any particular efficiency, and whose art is part of an attempt to facilitate or stabilize the process as they conceive it. Although the word "primitive" is thoroughly inoffensive in its literal meanings, it does imply our superiority and to many people brings an image of bone-in-the-nose unsophistication. A circumlocution such as "art of under-developed countries and lost civilizations" only proves that the longest way round is the longest way round.

Dr. Robert Goldwater, the director of the museum, a quiet man with an inward sparkle that he occasionally makes visible, reports that "indigenous art" was tried for a time, but no one knew what indigenous meant, so it was abandoned. Apparently no one tried the synonym for "indigenous," which would have resulted in "autoch-thonous art," a title with a fine primitive ring to it, especially with its arrow-shaped leading letter. The British favored the label "tribal art" for a time. One of the best names, according to Dr. Goldwater, is "art of preliterate peoples."

Obviously it is very difficult to get an inclusive or descriptive term. Much of this confusion is due to the vast range of "primitive art," which covers African, pre-Columbian, and Pacific cultures vastly different in their beliefs, customs, and sophistication. When more is known about them, some will doubtless separate themselves from the inclusive term "primitive art" and become well-defined separate areas of appreciation and study, just as much as other anonymous arts such as Gothic or Romanesque art. Thus the museum is in a pioneering position at the moment, coping with rapidly widening knowledge and with popular misconceptions about primitive art.

The museum is adamant about one thing. The criterion for an object's admission is its artistic worth. "However, we attempt to keep some balance between the pure aesthetic approach and the ethnological approach," Dr. Goldwater said.

Again, this is a pioneering and delicate course in primitive-art appreciation. Both ethnology, which looks on the art as a source of social information, and aesthetics, which has taught a generation of students to exclaim how much some African masks resemble Modiglianis, are entirely valid but limited approaches. Dr. Goldwater, however, favors a productive interaction between them, in which the visual aspect is primary but is qualified by "sufficient curiosity to find out the meaning of the object in its own culture." This is asking for no more than the usual approach of any student to an art new to him, but it is surprising how many feel that primitive art should be an exception to the usual method of approaching art, without giving any good reason why.

There is perhaps no art that makes so direct a visual impact as primitive art. This generalization applies particularly to the compressed and sudden rhythms of African art, and Dr. Goldwater has found African art the most popular when shown. Following this advantage with the qualifying information regarding rites, ritual, and cultural background is likely to be much more difficult.

First of all, a great deal of the information is simply not available, though considerable advances have been made recently in the chronology of African and Mexican art. Second, when the information is available it is quite likely to be of a nature that will turn the viewer against the object that so attracted him initially. Further acquaintance with Aztec customs, for instance, tends to turn the cultural gap between them and us into an abyss. It is bridged only by investigation into those areas of motivation and the subconscious that most of us are not anxious to uncover.

It is to the credit of the Museum of Primitive Art that it tackles these problems of appreciation, communication, and education quietly and efficiently, without beating what we have come to recognize as the usual museum drum.

June 1962
The New York Times

Maxim Karolik

HE IS A large, handsome, voluble, impossible man, with a fine head set on slightly hunched shoulders, a strong aquiline nose, hooded eyes, and large masculine ears. Two deep wrinkles place brackets around his wide mouth, and indeed around everything that comes out of it, for he is continually quoting authority which most frequently turns out to be himself.

He has the most eloquent forefinger in Boston, and one of the most eloquent since Michelangelo's "Creation of Adam." It is the thin end of an unstoppable wedge. When he gathers himself behind that finger and zeros in, one's imagination conjures up a solid wall in the air behind one's back. He pins you against your own imagination.

He takes particular care, in his absolutely precise Russian accent, to use words exactly according to their meaning. His attachment to precision of meaning and his attachment to an extraordinary venture of the imagination have exasperated many, bored some, pleased thousands, and filled some blank pages in American history.

The blank pages, like everything else, are precisely defined— 1815–1865—the least glamorized backwater in American history, when the country was consolidating its provincial position. It needed a Civil War to make America cosmopolitan.

These blank pages have been filled not with words, but with pictures—some of the most surprising, dreadful, magnificent, and happily sentimental pictures produced anywhere. Occupying four small galleries at the Boston Museum of Fine Arts, they make up the M. and M. Karolik Collection of American Paintings, 1815– 1865. The magnificent Maxim Karolik (his name or his person always enters with an imaginary roll of trumpets, for he has flair and color) initated this particular collection with his wife, Martha Codman Karolik, in 1939, and continued it after her death in 1948. With this collection the Karoliks splendidly filled what scholars had been pleased to call "a barren period" in American art. From the limbo of their chosen half-century, they recovered some of the finest pictures painted in America, rescued forgotten names, discovered piquant primitives, and scrupulously annotated their dream.

It was a dream sustained from its birth by an act of faith between the Boston Museum and the Karoliks, who entered the anonymous half-century like true explorers, wondering if there was anything there, but believing there was. Mr. Karolik must have been the first collector anywhere to offer a museum a collection that didn't exist and who then went out and got it. And since repetition of a good thing is deeply ingrained in his character he did this not once, but repeated it three times. There are three Karolik Collections. The American paintings were preceded by a collection of American furniture, and succeeded by a collection of American watercolors and drawings, with a few sculptures, of the nineteenth century, which opened in October and is now on view at the Museum of Fine Arts. These collections he calls "The Trilogy," and Mr. Karolik's eulogy of his trilogy is one of Boston's better performances. Like a play, it is repeated exactly.

He believes thoroughly in the value of art as a social and civilizing force. Through the collections, America recovers a lost part of its history, and, viewing itself in the mirror of its completed past, is surer of its identity. This aspect is deeply meaningful to Mr. Karolik. "Why," he said once, trying to bring this home to me, "the collections are even more important than—than Maxim Karolik." He paused for a moment as if overcome by the enormity of what he had said. Mr. Karolik is as remarkable as his and his late wife's collections.

This champion of a lost American art in a lost half-century is the unlikeliest champion imaginable. What passed between a Russian émigré and a few anonymous nineteenth-century American paintings back in 1942 when he first saw them is a mystery that I have not been able to solve. Why did he begin to collect what native Americans ignored or despised? What was it exactly that attracted him? Was it an impulse to recover a forgotten past in a new country, now that his own past was destroyed behind him? Mr. Karolik, whose silence can be as remarkable as his volubility, does not say.

His birthplace was in Bessarabia, something of a football in international politics. The Russians lost it to Rumania after Versailles. They got it back following the cynical Russo-German pact of August 1939 and the rape of Poland. The German panzers overran it when opening up the Eastern front two years later. Mr. Karolik's home town was called Akerman. The Russians gave it another name. The Nazis destroyed it. "They say even the cemetery was destroyed."

Mr. Karolik lived and studied for a while in Petrograd, spent some time in Kiev, and went to dramatic school in Odessa, where he studied with Savinov, the follower of Stanislavsky, who was killed during the revolution. But Mr. Karolik's ambition was to be an operatic tenor, and he is still fond of saying, "I am not a man but a tenor," presumably in tribute to the inhuman discipline singing demands.

He remembers his teachers with affection. "What teachers I had I value them now even more. When I was seventeen years old Savinov said 'It is people who live with dignity, with excellence, who matter.' The dignity I'm talking about does not require a stuffed shirt and a high hat, but comes from *within*, the dignity of thought, of feeling, of outlook. This is necessary in an enlightened democracy." Mr. Karolik was trained in the Tolstoy tradition, with a belief in the ennobling value of art. The Karolik Collection of paintings was rooted firmly in this belief.

The Bolsheviks took over in 1917. Mr. Karolik stayed one year. "I will not tell you what I saw. It is unbelievable. I tell you a revolution is good to see in the movies after a good dinner." After that he wandered over Europe, two years in Italy, seven months in London, part of a floating population that included such diverse talents as a prince who played brilliant football ("Do you know Obolenski?" "No, I am the spiritual type.") and a writer who turned English into a circus with himself as ringmaster. ("Did you know Nabokov?" "Ah, yes, the composer." "I didn't know he was a composer, I thought he wrote novels." "Well, the brother writes books, so sophisticated it's frightening—all head, and one about the little girl . . ." It was refreshing to hear Vladimir Nabokov identified through his brother.)

In 1922 Mr. Karolik, tinged with the glamor of Russian exile, arrived in America. He followed a brief career as a concert tenor, and in 1928 married Martha Codman of Boston. Now, thirty-five years later, his conquest of America's Athens is complete. Boston without Mr. Karolik is unthinkable. So is American art without the Karolik Collections.

When he and his wife were presenting the first collection to the Boston Museum, he wrote to George H. Edgell, then director, with the innocent and honest egoism that characterizes his letters. "Our dream is becoming a reality. Our aim was to collect the very best America created in the Fine Arts in the 18th and 19th centuries. We have succeeded, I believe. This collection" he went on, "in our opinion, represents the ARTIST, whose creative work reflects the taste of an epoch.

"In full sobriety, without false modesty or bombastic pride, I say to you: My wife and I realize the importance of our collection, the value of which lies in the Social, Aesthetic, Cultural, and Educational meaning of it."

The firm capitalizations and personifications are very much in keeping with his nineteenth-century regard for the social and moral values of art. The people staring fixedly out of the portraits included in the first collection would have understood Mr. Karolik and his prose completely. The first four portraits in that first collection include the Winslows, like Mr. Karolik émigrés after revolution, and the John Amorys. Something Mrs. Amory (Martha Codman Karolik's great-great-grandmother) wrote in her journal after her passage to England would please Mr. Karolik very much:

"Went on shore Saturday June 24th, about 9 o'clock in the morning. After dinner, went to view the cathedral—Our Senses were ravish'd with Wonder & Delight in beholding the ancient and noble Structure & thought that the sight of this alone, fully repaid us for our Sea Sickness." The capitalizations are Karolikian. So is the firm sense of ennoblement before art. People make themselves worthy of art, and since Art is for the people, this is a form of enlightened democracy which, when first advocated by Mr. Karolik, was, he remembers, received as a form of socialism.

"When I mentioned the Aesthetic and Historic values at the Boston Museum when we were getting started, everything was fine. But Sociological—and I felt the temperature drop. I selected this museum to reach the people. But the dowagers asked 'What does he mean by that? Is he pink or red?'" The late George H. Edgell, however, who was then director, well understood. He wrote in his foreword to the first collection: "It is a gift not for the glorification of the donors, not for the enrichment of the Museum of Fine Arts, not for the elite and sophisticated in art, but for the common people of the nation."

Art as a social and civilizing force is one of Mr. Karolik's deepest beliefs, and it rides grandly over the modern suspicion of literary values in art. He is extremely critical of the cliché that art is a sort of spiritual tranquilizer to be fed the masses. The modern museum trend to sell art at the lowest common denominator of entertainment provokes him to baroque gestures and eloquence.

"What is the purpose of a museum?" he says. "You come to a museum to feel finer, not better. To feel better we need only a good steak, to feel finer we need more than that. A museum is an ideal, not a reality. Science is practical, a Museum of Fine Arts is an ideal. I am a collector driven by ideas, not by a hobby. A museum serves the community not as an entertainment. You shouldn't sell the fine arts like Coca-Cola and soap. It offends me to be invited to relax and have a good time. No, a real museum lifts the public to the level of the museum, not brings the museum down to them. A museum preserves high standards and the meaning of the fine arts—reverence for excellence, for creativity, for genuineness. That's the meaning of the word education. You educate not for the sake of teaching, but for enlightenment. If you want to be taught you go to an academy, not to a museum. The word 'museum' has a lofty meaning. You cannot just say 'Come in, enjoy togetherness.' A museum cannot have a motto like a department store. Directors who want to entertain with exhibition all the time, they are not directors, they are exhibitionists!"

Thus Mr. Karolik places himself finally between the two conflicting museum trends—conservation of treasures for the future, and education of the masses by means of them today. He has great delight in finding his views substantiated in all sorts of places. "Malraux," he said to me once with finger and eyebrows raised, "Malraux—there are passages in which he quotes me." He was thoroughly delighted when Henry Rossiter of the Boston Museum brought to his attention a forgotten book, *Art in the United States* (1852) by a forgotten writer, George Washington Bethune. "A hundred years before the Collection, he wrote and said what *I* am saying," said Mr. Karolik. Bethune spoke of the "happy monument" that nineteenth-century American art might some day have.

That "happy monument" is most truly visible in the middle—and most famous—Karolik Collection, the paintings. They show a new landscape and a new society being shaped, with a sort of premature Victorianism, into some of America's most touching documents.

The Trilogy, with the opening of the Water Colors and Drawings Collection, is ended. Looking over the twenty-seven years in which it dominated his thoughts, Mr. Karolik in his final letter to the Boston Museum emphasized again what it had meant to him, quoting liberally from his letters in the two previous catalogues.

Even more so, however, an article published twenty years ago (October, 1942) in *The Atlantic Monthly* shows clearly where Mr. Karolik's sympathies and beliefs lie. He wrote then: "I believe that the people who came here during the 17th and 18th centuries did not intend to continue the way of life they left behind them. They were longing for something new, something better. The epoch-making Declaration of Independence shows what they were longing for: freedom of worship, freedom of speech, and freedom of assembly. They also dreamed of equality of opportunity. This desire has been called the American dream. The concept that all men are born equal was to the men of 1776 no mere phrase, no mere flight of fancy; it was their blueprint of American Destiny. It implied a deep faith in the common man, and it expressed a determination to give him equality of opportunity. It was America's unique contribution to history."

This miracle has always dazzled Mr. Karolik's eyes. At times he has felt that the practical ideals of the country's founders have been sadly obscured by some of their successors. "When I came to this country . . . I was astonished to find that [the practical business-man] had little in common with the type of man who created the Declaration of Independence. To him, I noticed, these men were sentimental dreamers, impractical idealists." The country's fathers, he wrote, "knew the simple longings of human nature: a comfortable home—the only place where intimate contentment can be reached; happiness, which comes from the realization that one is free to express himself. They knew that grandiose enterprises and colossal achievements are of no use if they add nothing to the good, the simple, elemental virtues."

Here for the first time we find some clue as to what went on in Mr. Karolik's head when he saw his first nineteenth-century American paintings. His was a mind instilled with the spirit of the country's founders. He had studied their times, their thoughts, their practical ideals, their Spartan virtues of simplicity and rectitude. Coming from a country laid waste by the tyrannical abuse of power, Mr. Karolik saw all this with the clarity of a man with new eyes. In the few paintings he first saw, these virtues were practically realized, an ideal made real on the canvas, because they were made real in the life around them. For Mr. Karolik hopes, and believes, that the Karolik Collections will realize his practical ideal as the men of 1776 realized theirs—that "it will help create a society in which human beings feel free and equal, in which ability in different fields is respected and honored, a society in which an aristocracy, if it should exist, is an aristocracy of mind and spirit. Such a society, called true democracy, was the dream of many great minds centuries ago."

This is the inspiration of the three Karolik Collections and of Mr. Karolik. Again and again he has emphasized that he has not just been a collector donating to a museum, but a practical idealist giving the people a collection that recovered their past, personified its ideals, and which can help shape their future. To see this in 1942 required great vision, and the Karolik Collections are a monument to one of this country's very few visionaries in the field of American art.

Winter 1962
Art in America

Huntington Hartford I: His Museum

SITUATED like an architectural afterthought on an oversized traffic island in Columbus Circle, New York, the Huntington Hartford Gallery of Modern Art has been a question mark on the New York art scene since it started getting itself born two years ago.

Since its patron and founder is known for his resolute opposition to any abstraction and for his love of painters long considered passé, it was expected to become the home of ultraconservatism, a sort of aesthetic John Birch Society.

The new gallery, however, couldn't have chosen a better time to be born, for taste has been changing and fashion flirting with the passé and the moribund. Some of the plans announced by the director, Carl J. Weinhardt, Jr., sound almost avant-garde, which all goes to prove the cyclical theory of taste. If you lag behind far enough, for long enough, history will catch up with you, pushing you along in front of it. Thus an institution that has seemed (often simultaneously) an eccentricity, a laughingstock, and an anachronism, has the opportunity of becoming an important addition to the New York scene, filling a gap that has been yawning wider and wider.

The first notice of policy was issued last week. Mr. Weinhardt announced that the program would be oriented "toward certain relatively neglected phases of nineteenth- and twentieth-century art." Two exhibitions were announced—a Tchelitchew retrospective (a passable enough middle-of-the-road decision) and a Pre-Raphaelite show put together by the Herron Art Museum in Indianapolis.

The Pre-Raphaelite show is a coup. For years, anyone who had a good word to say for this mid-nineteenth-century group of sentimental anti-industrialists was considered either a Victorian hangover or simply some sort of nut. But the Pre-Raphaelites have been coming back into favor, part of a revival of interest in the nineteenth century in its widest contexts. In mounting this show, the new gallery can happily hunt with the conservative hounds and run with the avant-garde hare, something it will have to make a career of doing.

By bringing in an out-of-town exhibition that normally wouldn't be seen here, the new gallery is filling a needed function. Last year (1962), the superb Barbizon show bypassed New York on its way from Toledo to Boston, which mightn't have happened had the Hartford Gallery been in operation.

Since the most vital force in twentieth-century art has undoubtedly been abstraction, it has retroactivated only such art as is ancestor to it, conversely depressing anything that is not, including a lot of more-or-less worthwhile nineteenth-century painting needing exploration, especially in its historical context. The Whitney Museum of American Art opted out of the nineteenth century in 1949. That leaves the Museum of Modern Art and the Guggenheim, both of whose policies include anything from about 1800 on if its relevance to the present can be established. Both, especially the Museum of Modern Art, are devoted to historical perspectives rather than to the historical context, *i.e.*, to the uses of the past to illuminate the present (and vice versa) rather than to a study of a section of the past in its immediate historical context. Both are entirely defensible interpretations of history. The point is, however, that the "perspective" view has been pretty exclusive in New York, and there is room for a "context" view of the past, which is presumably what the Hartford Gallery will provide. At the same time it will provide a focus for the few commercial galleries (e.g., Drawing Shop, Lewison Gallery, Robert S. Sloan's) that have been alone in defining the new development in taste.

The Hartford Gallery, according to Mr. Weinhardt, takes as "modern" anything after 1800, which leaves it with an *embarras de richesse* up to about 1900 and an *embarras de pauvreté* after, since abstraction, as a matter of policy, is out ("Abstraction is done very well elsewhere in the city," says Mr. Weinhardt). Thus twentieth-century art for the Hartford Gallery must of necessity become a question of taking second-best moderns much as Tchelitchew, or of bringing in academic hacks from the outer darkness, or of displaying first-class moderns such as Hopper, Wyeth, and Burchfield, which, once done, leaves the cupboard bare. Obviously the gallery is going to make its major contributions in the nineteenth-century field, which is where the big gap is, notably in American art.

That nineteenth-century American art is in the position of a poor relation in this country is a surprise to any foreigner, since it provides insights into America you can't get any other way, and since it often ranks highly as art. Apart from the Metropolitan's dutiful nod, and the New-York Historical Society contemplating its frozen and valuable collections, it receives virtually no attention in this city, especially since two leading explorers (Messrs. Goodrich and Baur of the Whitney) have been diverted to the twentieth century. There is no place you can see a Bierstadt or Quidor retrospective, for instance, no place for a show of Harnett and his circle. Here the Hartford Gallery can become a vitally functioning and necessary part of the American scene and earn something it has had a hard time getting—respect.

Outside the American nineteenth century, unmentionables now becoming mentionable (groups like the Nazarenes, names like G. F. Watts and Meissonier) need another look to see just how good or bad they are (the Royal Academy put on a Landseer show a few years ago on the principle that he could not be that bad. He was).

That is about the situation as it stands. A museum expected to be superfluous may have a vital function. Its nineteenth-century performance could be definitive. Its twentieth-century performance is limited and fraught with hazards. By chance, the new gallery arrives at an opportune historical moment. Its history will largely be the record of whether it grasped that moment or not.

January 1964
The New York Times

Huntington Hartford II: His Book

HUNTINGTON HARTFORD is an average millionaire who reportedly dreams of the day when someone will mention his name without immediately adding "A & P heir." To remove this commercial taint, he has devoted himself to the arts, a field in which millionaires traditionally have had dreams of glory. He has made two solid contributions—*Show* Magazine, which he has just sold, and the Gallery of Modern Art, which he has shoe-horned into Columbus Circle in New York. The main threat to both these successes is Huntington Hartford. He keeps giving them the benefit of his ideas.

These ideas have free play in his new book, *Art or Anarchy?* (Doubleday), which has finally struggled upward through layers of publishers and editors, many of whom have left their mark, so that reading it is like excavating a historical site. Hartford making like a thinker is first-class entertainment, a disarming parable of incompetent goodwill. His heart is always in the right place. It's his head that's in trouble.

The subtitle of the book sounds more eighteenth than twentieth century: "How the extremists and exploiters have reduced the fine arts to chaos and commercialism." Much of the book seems written from the eighteenth century too, with occasional courageous advances into the nineteenth. He tries to make a case against abstract art (at this stage like trying to repeal the New Deal), against obscurity in art and criticism (although critics and artists are devoted just now to precision and clarity), and—along with other things—against the corruptions of the art market. There is a case to be made on the last score, but Hartford hasn't the slightest idea how to distinguish invention from fashion, avant-garde from pseudo-avant-garde, the rich and ignorant patron from the true connoisseur. He resents—as many of us do—the intrusion of big money (and consequently of human nature) into the business of the fine arts, a mixed blessing which he mixes a bit more. He is a black-and-white person for whom true and false are as separate as the answers in the TV quiz show. For a social critic this is an antiquated attitude unless it generates the excitement of literate prejudice. Hartford has plenty of prejudices, but none of them are literate. He shows how an inept attack automatically switches around to a good defense of what he is attacking.

What does Hartford believe in? Hold onto your seat as we push forward into the nineteenth century. ". . . There must be a certain subject or subject matter which the artist wishes to paint and which both he and the viewers can recognize. From this point he must take us by the hand, figuratively, and lead us into the realm of the beautiful, the ideal—into the realm of the emotions."

To push through this thesis he conscripts a team of motley giants and puts them into action like a football squad—left guard, Goya; center, da Vinci; right tackle, Tolstoy; right end, John Dewey, etc. He quarterbacks this team of good guys against the bad guys, nasty people like John Osborne, Picasso ("The greatest mountebank in the history of art"), the dealer Sidney Janis, Tennessee Williams, T. S. Eliot, Willem de Kooning, and assorted infamies such as "the beatnik, the Existentialist, the juvenile delinquent, the zaniest of abstract art, the weirdest aberrations of the mentally unbalanced, the do-nothing philosophy of pseudo-Zen Buddhism"—all the results of the abuse of freedom and liberty. Hartford calls a lot of signals, but his all-star team won't budge.

At this stage, if you haven't suspected it already, you discover that Hartford is a moralist. What sort of moralist? Well, what he likes is moral and what he doesn't like is immoral. "The outward and visible sign of this morality in the case of a painting is the subject matter." Abstraction is immoral and dangerous. Who pushed American abstraction? The Communists, of course, to weaken our moral fiber.

But the fun is only beginning. Things fall into place. Mr. Hartford is suspicious of intelligence. "It is the complex individuals—" here he fingers the artist—"who tend to keep a philosophy of bitterness alive in the world." One page later he has decided that the artist is "the most generous and gullible of souls . . ." Later he's a psychopath, still later maybe he isn't.

The book was written before the election. One begins to suspect that Hartford might have been tapped as Minister for Culture in Barry Goldwater's cabinet. His thundering sermon comes complete with exhortations to return to the simple, decent life, with simple old formulas to apply to complex new problems, with built-in nostalgia for a Currier & Ives Utopia. One can't finish this marvelously archaic opus without developing an affection for it. A Trea-

sury of Inanities, a Layman's Guide to Obsolete Prejudices, it is not
to be missed by any connoisseur of the absurd.

November 1964
Life

New York and the New Whitney Museum

THE MAJOR EVENT of the New York season took place on
September 28 when the Whitney Museum of American Art re-
opened at its new location on Madison Avenue and 75th Street. The
Whitney thus removed itself from its uneasy proximity to the
Museum of Modern Art on 54th Street, where since 1954 they had
existed side by side, with connecting doors—a leading example of
Siamese twins with nothing in common but their physical bond.
You could hardly speak of one without the other, and physical
proximity prompted unconditional comparisons. Thus the Whitney
—poorer, occupying a dull, leaden building, short of staff and with a
totally opposite approach to art—was continually measured against
the Modern Museum's consummate performances.

Now outside the Modern Museum's glamorous aura, the
Whitney has its first reasonable chance to clarify its catholic and
unfashionable approach to a scene in which partisanship and fashion are major forces. If properly articulated and carried out, the
Whitney's approach contains, I believe, the philosophy most applicable to the current scene. For nearly a decade of virtually
prepackaged innovation and novelty has produced a certain museum illness, a malaise that affects the other three museums—the
Modern, the Guggenheim, and perhaps the Jewish—to a greater or
lesser extent. For there is a crisis of avant-gardism, and thus a major
crisis among the museums devoted to it. So the opening of the new

Whitney leads one to question our routine assumptions about the existence and function of modern museums ("modern" has become a very old-fashioned word); it leads us into theories of the historical present, and into the nature of art now. But first, the new museum itself.

Marcel Breuer, its architect, writes of "the attempt to form the building itself as a sculpture." If we accept this, the Whitney is undoubtedly the season's major one-man show. An inverted ziggurat, it steps up and out in three deep ledges from the Madison Avenue side. The solid elephant-gray facing is relieved by a large window, rather low on the topmost bank. Six other windows are arbitrarily disposed on the 75th Street side. All the windows have the same trapezoidal tilt. The entrance, across a bridge, gives views down to a basement sculpture garden which communicates with the basement galleries through large plate-glass windows. Inside, the three major gallery floors increase in length as one goes up. The topmost floor, the fifth, is the administration area; generously windowed offices face a corridor of space which is abruptly closed off by a blank wall—the inside of the frontage extended upward to preserve the monolithic look from outside.

To take the obvious merits first: The endemic Manhattan problem of limited outdoor space is met by undercutting the solid block of building and sinking the sculpture garden. This ingenious plaza-substitute gives some sense of outward motion and activity as people scurry and drift under the raised edge of what feels like an enormous boulder. It's an original solution, rather like an exaggerated Cubist version of the Guggenheim's spinning "top." The effect, with the rather dour granite frontage and the top-heavy downward thrust, is a powerful one that dispenses with easy grace and elegance. The ziggurat comes down like a pile driver, and one looks over the street wall to see how far into the ground the building has driven itself. Having forced attention so unambiguously downward, the sculpture garden and basement galleries have to sustain an intended focus, which they do reasonably well, although the descending sense of quarrylike gloom tends to cramp the space so ingeniously and dearly bought.

From the outside, the building has great distinction, although one could quarrel with it interminably. The windows, whose tilted axes are seasonably apt in that they resemble some of the constructions in fashion this year, make reasonably good connections between inside and out—though a case could be made that, like avant-garde portholes on a block of meteorite, they attempt to alleviate and cosmeticize a problem rather than solve it. The main fault from the outside, to me, is the ineffectiveness of the bridge with its concrete flap cantilevered over the sidewalk. As a balance to the overhanging ziggurat it is fragile and contrived, and it blurs the main structure. But in its splendid absence of chic, its powerful utilitarian statement of purpose, its bold main idea, the building is impressive and successful.

The taciturn quality of the outside is carried into the interior with further modulations of gray—light-gray walls, flagged (and stiletto-heel-resistant) floors—although one wood-paneled gallery seems to detach itself sharply from the main idea to cultivate a Danish modern tastefulness at odds with the building. But the great interior problems of space and light have been solved (or successfully passed on) with results allowing virtually frightening flexibility. The concrete "egg-crate" ceilings bear on their free edges and multiple intersections devices for lighting and wall suspension, and thus hand on to the curator the major problems of deciding how to rebuild the museum for each show—something that will demand considerable virtuosity.

This heavy, loculated ceiling of rectangular "cells" again carries through the sense of high specific gravity, the downward pull that seems to pervade the entire structure with the exception of the airy fifth floor. The ceiling may bear down a bit on paintings that come close, but the major gallery, at 17½ feet, has plenty of height, and my guess is that the ceiling will turn out to be one of those obvious features that quickly tend to be ignored by habit.

The lighting system throughout is daring. The entrance hall (unaccountably broken by a granite bench) has a ceiling seeded with high-intensity lights; reflected down from touching discs that look like an electric water-lily pond, the light can stun the gloomy entrance with brightness, which can be controlled by rheostat. In fact, it is this contrast of lighting potential with architectural weight and gloom that is the building's most provocative interior feature. Two last points—one inside, one out. Some will quarrel with the corridor of space around the fifth floor. Ostensibly a place for storing sculpture, it leaves numerous windows numbly looking out on the blank wall necessary for outward consistency. And the attempt to "frame" the building with two projecting end walls of equal height seems a suspect way of controlling the environment rather than entering into some kind of dialogue with it.

Finally, and most importantly, the building exists to show works of art. I feel that here it is a major success, if close attention is given to display. It should work very well as a museum, for it has a responsibility to the art it contains that is exactly opposite the Guggenheim's eccentric hostility.

The Whitney makes its move uptown (physically countering the shift of the art world's center of gravity down toward 57th Street over the past few seasons) during a time that may be remembered as "The Crisis of the Museums." For the Guggenheim and Modern Museum are contemplating their own images with considerable insecurity. The Modern, having lost brilliant middle-aged men, and apparently afraid of brilliant young men, seems to be in an overdiversified catatonic sprawl. It has so successfully followed its vanguard course, so carefully educated a vast audience, and acquired so splendidly, that it seems to have removed its reason for existence as a "modern" museum; each day it looks more and more like a satellite of the Metropolitan Museum.

It is a victim of its own theory of history, the idea of avant-gardism as a permanent phenomenon, with all its attendant assumptions. Now these assumptions are suspect, and art is a social profession, not an antisocial phenomenon. The Modern has favored the "perspective" view, in which the dominant mode or moment opens a single historical corridor. Recently Turner, in a typical reverse ancestry, has been legitimized by the color painters. This is fine, once the idea of avant-gardism is historically viable. Now the dominant moment has been split, has become incredibly labile. Any attempt to follow it equipped only with a theory of history as progress, such as avant-gardism essentially is, can only lead to frustration and paralysis, or to attempts at false dialecticism and syntheses in "art history."

This is where the new Whitney, traditionally called "dull" in the midst of all the swingers (and an easy target all of us have had a go at, at one time or another), comes in. It has an opportunity to prove that dullness in this context is almost a virtue, and that it is capable of elaborating its catholicity into a theory of history applicable to the complexities of a rapidly diversifying present. The Whitney's future depends on whether it can pioneer an aesthetic shift back from competitive avant-gardism to less spectacular but more apt examinations of "contexts." The closest the Whitney has come to formally articulating this purpose was in 1961 when Lloyd Goodrich and John I. H. Baur (the museum's director and associate director) wrote in *American Art of Our Century*: "Contemporary American art is extremely diverse, and this calls for a broad viewpoint, recognizing all creative tendencies from traditional to advanced. . . . It should never forget that the artist is the prime mover in all artistic matters." How can this be made an aggressive, positive position?

For this, one has, I think, to venture into the jungle of ideas in which theories of history are debated, theories that art history seems never to have heard of. One of the major paradoxes about art history as an academic discipline is that it has virtually no theory of history. It avoids one by iconographical proliferation (e.g., "The Clown Theme in Early Twentieth-Century Art") or by formal dialectics (e.g., "The Development of the Biomorphic Form in

Arp"). The former is, historically speaking, usually naïve; the latter is founded on questionable aesthetics, just as "stylistic development" is part of what Karl Popper would call the fallacy of historicism. For art "historians" one might recommend a gentle dose of slightly disturbing historians such as Marc Bloch or Lucien Febvre to question their assumptions; then any book that cancels the idea of progress (e.g., Ernest Lee Tuveson's *Millennium and Utopia*); and follow up hard with, say, Popper on *The Poverty of Historicism*.

Then one might at least be in a position to redefine history and reinterpret its apparent inevitability. One would be free to reconstruct alternatives, point out *how rejected alternatives affect the course taken*, and how the course taken intersects at the next "nodal" point of decision where other variables converge and other alternatives fan out. This careful reconstruction of "contexts," combined with an almost surgical delicacy in separating and reconnecting past and present, contributes to an idea of history suitable to a present that has not "broken down," but simply has broken out of the framework in which we habitually see it. The only major exhibition in which some of these ideas were taken into account was the Baltimore Museum's broad cross-section "1914" which included only works of all kinds produced that year.

Yet, surprisingly, one discovers that this is exactly what the Whitney has been pointing toward in its own way. It has carefully cultivated figures such as Burlin, Zerbe, and Dickinson to contribute to the broad tissue of history, carefully handled the past without distorting it to prove some aspect of the present, and in its Annuals catalogued, at the expense of a single dialectical development, numerous traditions, including those considered obsolete. With something of a shock, one realizes that the Whitney is now in a position to offer more than the Modern Museum. The Whitney's next step must be, I feel, into some kind of "structuralist" criticism that has helped revivify some other disciplines, notably anthropology. As Mark Slonim defined it recently, there is a shift from "emphasizing ideological or economic determinants to a search for systems of relationships, for conventional patterns and intrinsic factors of change and development." Applied to the present by a museum, it demands a tremendous concentration of critical thinking. The possibilities are immense, and might help dislodge our concept of a modern museum, which has simply never got rid of the nineteenth-century idea of a museum as society's custodian for alienated and extruded precious objects. Now the split that gave rise to such a concept is breaking down, and with it there is stress on these modern museum walls.

There are other good signs at the Whitney. It has returned to pre-1900 American art; since 1949 it had limited itself to post-1900. It has quietly developed a conditional method for getting rid of obsolete art, thus trying to develop an evacuation system in the frozen museum storerooms. It is girding itself to handle, through the vast civil service of the arts that is developing in the United States from Federal to local levels, the problems of bringing art to the aesthetically underdeveloped areas.

Here again the Whitney is better equipped to deal with the problem than the Modern. The Modern has continually sent avant-garde and international exhibitions to the continental stretches of the interior, where they have frequently caused confusion and augmented provincialism. This presumes a homogeneous America— which is simply advertising's convention or propaganda. The Whitney, placing its shows carefully with respect to local conditions, is aware that aesthetically this continent is like Africa politically. The Whitney's implicit concept of a diffused historical present, within which varying levels of development and clarification occur, is exactly suited to the real situation, and the Whitney has a great opportunity to make the next decade its own. As a place from which to manipulate into this future, the Whitney's powerful, opaque, and charmless new building seems exactly right.

October 1966
Art and Artists

PART THREE

THEMES
AND FUTURES

Criticizing Criticism

A MAIN THREAT to modern art seems to have gone unrecognized—the people who write about it. For art now has a problem it never had before. It is being overinterpreted, overcriticized, and overdocumented in a strangling undergrowth of verbal redundancies.

One great error has been the injudicious application of ponderous academic methodologies—fostering overspecialization and pedantry—to the humanities. Now the universities show signs of taking over modern art in a way that they (and the New Criticism) took over poetry a few decades ago, and the results have a similar suspicious look.

The *Kunstgeschichte* of the specialists pays off large rewards when applied to the right area. Its application to modern art is, to say the least of it, doubtful. It is, of course, difficult to refute this take-over, since the method's *raison d'être* is so logically correct, and is, in fact, a valuable triumph of methodology that turned art history into a rewarding scholarly discipline. But the reduction of the humanities to scientific logic has often been one of the critical disasters of the twentieth century, just as sentimental imprecision was often one of the critical disasters of the nineteenth.

The specialization that isolates a part from the whole, a necessary standard procedure in the sciences, often leads quickly to the ridiculous in the arts, especially when it is a modern art—one watches in awe as the *kunsthistorische* methodology, one of the shining glories of scholarship, a sort of theoretical IBM machine running on facts, is applied to Pop art.

This methodology obtains its best results when applied to a past more or less fixed by natural selection and evolution. When applied to the contemporary scene by eager young pedants, it wraps up what is fluid and changing in a sort of deadening scholarly insulation.

Enough of the results are in for one to suspect that modern art may be in the process of becoming an adjunct to the writer—a bizarre inversion of value. Painting is being produced (as has already been well said by Saul Steinberg) for critics and scholars just as poetry up to a few years ago was being produced by professors for other professors to analyze *ad nauseam*.

Take, for instance, *Art International*, a magazine that does what it sets out to do so well that it is totally depressing. One cannot read an issue completely without feeling an intense malaise. The reason is that this magazine, which has a fondness for some of the worst aspects of the *kunsthistorische* mentality, notably its humorless seriousness (people can be humorous *and* serious), is one of the spiritual vacuums through which art is made to pass, being denatured in the process to a sort of in-group party. It short-circuits the life-enhancing properties of art to make it a dead appendage to society.

One recent article took an artist of decidedly limited performance and gave him the method treatment—relating him to tradition, providing him with parents and issue, footnoting with impressive erudition, ending up with an article as impassive and loveless as a wall. It was a brilliant article within its limits, but the author seemed unaware of what these limits do to the article and to contemporary art. This sort of thing (the opposite of the *Art News* depth psychology that makes criticism a dense parallel to the artist's creation—preferable because it is based on some poetic intuition, however crude) freezes the current scene into a graveyard, planting a tombstone neatly over every artist with his code number and case history engraved on it. A living artist's work, which is essentially fluid and variable—and must be kept so—is quickly fixed into a straitjacket of academic "examination." It's a good artist who can get out of that one, especially when the fitting of the straitjacket is an act of flattery.

Why such magazines and such an approach to modern art exist is, of course, a question that leads right out of art into sociology, a route many important questions in art take nowadays. Since the economics of overpopulation has invaded the art field, these magazines are consumers for the vast army of people on their way to, or in, the colleges across the country, seeking advancement as best they can. In the academic world young scholars in all fields are faced with the problems of living and fighting their way up under one of the strangest banners ever devised. Called "Publish or Perish," it makes advancement subject to quantity rather than quality of publication—the mentality of an academic Woolworth's, something worth an article in itself.

Thus the academic world, the world of *kunsthistorische* methodology, is now moving into modern art with majestic and deadening dullness, and this academic world is subject to the same economic squeeze that makes our society produce other artificial markets for surplus. Most of the writing in the art field is surplus. The academic method as applied to modern art is certainly producing a lot of that surplus, and it has its dangers, since it misunderstands the nature of history and of modern art.

The effect of this overdocumentation on taste is a serious problem that someone has yet to tackle. Again the process of what one might call natural selection is tampered with. It is being replaced by an artificial selective process that gives big names to nonentities who are merely vehicles or avatars for scholars on the way up. By throwing the deadening weight of academism at anything new— look what happened to abstract expressionism: from loft to Ph.D. thesis in one concussive blow—originality is cut off from its sources of life and killed with academic kindness. And history is frozen too early into patterns that interfere with its natural evolution.

As well as being a problem for the present, pedantry and academism in modern criticism may be forcing on us the sort of artist we will get, since it is setting up false expectations that will affect the future. It is quite possible that we could have a series of artificial movements produced by artists unaware of the lethal effect of the academic writer in their midst, providing for these writers the raw material for their depressingly exhaustive theses, thus getting the art-writing industry into as healthy an economic shape as the New Criticism literary industry was in its heyday.

This prospect is one of the most depressing things in sight. It is time to recognize its morbid potential. One of the most ironic ways in which it realizes that potential is by establishing a liaison with the public-relations aspect of promotion and selling. What can be more "genuine" or respectable than a *kunsthistorische* job on an artist spread out quietly on the gallery table? The universities seem to be making their first, perhaps involuntary, liaison with high fashion. Perhaps someone can take it up from right here, with an article on "The Pedant as Christian Dior."

November 1963
The New York Times

The Corruption of Individuality

IT IS DIFFICULT to criticize the effects of big business without appearing slightly paranoid, but it is on record that in recent years the visual arts have drawn the type of speculator more usually found in movies, the stock market, and advertising. This has created a false climate around the artist, adding one more element of self-consciousness to the paralyzing number he already has to cope with.

It has also created something entirely new in modern art—the "hot" property. And the hot property, a money-maker, is the total prisoner of his success, and can be managed, coerced, pressured and discarded as if art were a type of show business. The new twist to the exploitation of the fashionable seems to be a result of pressures created by mass interest and big-business interest in the arts.

In fact, it is the prospect of such success that seems to draw many young artists to their profession. It is not unusual nowadays to hear a young artist talk—like a young actor—of "making it." Judging from some of the letters and photographs that arrive in this office [at *The New York Times*], one would think some young artists were trying to launch stage careers. Their work is apparently the vehicle for their ambition, not an end in itself. Their criterion of success is a write-up in *Time* Magazine or pictures in *Life*. Adding to the melancholy of these meditations is the memory of the number of shows last season in which good artists (from previous performances) sold out. Again, selling out is nothing new, but doing so with an air of preserving integrity is.

This displacement of ambition from the work to the career is, in New York, virtually accepted as normal. The pull is on the artist to become, even against his will, a sort of activist who has to sell himself as well as his work. And the pull is on the middleman (the gallery owner or dealer) to compete in selling the product by means of the usual devices of businessmen.

Caught up in the artificial forces of big business, the artist is having a hard time being his own man. He is under pressure from the public, the dealer, the collector, and the critic. He must create under false, but accepted, notions that confuse originality with innovation. He is expected to conform to ideas of individuality that are not his own. From all this has come what might be called "the corruption of individuality"—giving the illusion of being different while being very much the same.

Thus, during the past season one frequently saw the spuriously "original" show devoted to a single idea or motif pursued to exhaustion, or, less politely, the gimmick. I remember a show of mailboxes (elegantly painted), another of frankfurters, and others manipulating primary motifs (egg shapes, circles, triangles, etc.) with a bright and anxious emptiness.

Such specialization encourages total recall of an artist by an easily identifiable tag—the "mailboxes man" or the "blue dots man." Individuality is ready-made in ways acceptable to a new semi-educated public.

The attention-getting device is nothing new in art. But its current frequency in the hothouse, big-money atmosphere is new. Thus it is time to clear the lines and define the real artist's position when that position is open to deceptions that many have unconsciously accepted.

The honest pursuit of excellence in art is stringent and demanding, and its rewards are usually not monetary. Since the standards of the genuine artist are self-made, he must go through private tortures to close the gap between performance and an ideal only he can see. There is no room for compromise with the world around him or with himself. Since there is a great deal of the anarchist in every genuine creator, society is more or less his natural enemy. He is engaged in breaking its rules to contribute to a new definition of individual freedom within society. Now especially, when the world has shrunk to the proportions of an overcrowded golf ball and standards are becoming malleable, we need the dissenter and the stimulation of meeting the challenge he provides. Up to now the role of the modern artist has been that of the great individual, the rebellious member of society, keeping that body irritable and alive through his dissent.

In New York, so often described with naïve parochialism as "the art center of the world," big business, with its attendant publicity, is producing a set of forces that replaces individuality with a synthetic substitute. The artist is at last having a role provided for him in society—that of the engaging but controllable oddball, playing happily with his bricks in the corner, on display to visitors—a sort of "artist in residence" to society.

Since big money in the arts is here to stay, let us hope that its current attempt to rape the artist will result in a future breed less liable to seduction. If not, art may well become another packaged product, with the artist on the assembly line gulled into thinking he's an individual in possession of his freedom.

June 1963
The New York Times

Art—or Whatever You Call It

ONE OF THE MOST MEMORABLE STATEMENTS I ever heard I heard at secondhand. A friend reported that a friend of his, a critic, on being told of some new art that looked good, said, "I don't care if it's good art, tell me if it's avant-garde."

The sentence may provide you, as it did me, with a text for meditation during the boredoms of travel. Now, finally, through overcontemplation, I have gotten to the core of the statement. There's a lot of truth in it, especially if you drop most of it, and come up with, "I don't care if it's art."

This offers a ready-made answer to those who ask at every opportunity the magic question, "Yes, but is it art?" They demand judgment by reference to some hidden scale of values they cannot see, but have pathetic faith that you do.

So, in accordance with the smartest philosophic practice we can tell the "Is it art?" people that the answer to their question is that they have been asking the wrong question. On the evidence of the past season, asking "Is it art?" is simply out of date. We are in a period of transition during which traditional redefinitions of art are being remade because they have become inadequate.

The telescoped movements, discoveries, and ideas of the past half-century did seem to have a critical key—a rigorous belief in pure form as a measuring rod. However, the formal approach is no longer the philosopher's stone that it at one time appeared to be. Some

199

current manifestations are difficult to judge by this standard, or, failing by it abysmally, remain somehow provocative. The critic is forced to realize that though he may maintain standards, he doesn't fundamentally make them. Some new works demand new standards, which those works implicitly offer.

When new standards are in process of evolution, a lot of bad work is passed along with the good, which is what happened in the ascendancy of Abstract Expressionism. When the standards solidified, the bad work naturally took a heavy, and sometimes necessary, beating. The good work created the standards and passed them.

Last season the "Is it art?" question often seemed particularly irrelevant. Even as defined by twentieth-century standards, concepts of art are changing. With Cubism and Futurism, structure and movement were potentially realized. Now they are actually realized. The distinction between painting and sculpture as separate media often no longer holds. Each takes on characteristics of the other, with the division between them often indistinguishable. Frequently wired for light and sound, art, like movies, has gone beyond the silent picture. In the twilight zone between art and theater is the Happening—an occurrence which, according to one of its leading impresarios, will have justified itself if it breaks down current assumptions of what art should be.

These developments, in summary, invade the fourth dimension of time—by motion, sound, and interrupted light. This involves what appears to be a new awareness of space—not the characteristic space of earlier twentieth-century painting and sculpture, but what might be called the everyday space occupied by the observer. Up to the recent past, the work of art and the observer occupied separate worlds, and one of the prime tenets of modern art was that "art and nature are separate." Now there is a tendency for the art object and the observer to share the environment in a sort of positive interaction that minimizes the distinction between art and life, and in fact affirms a new relationship between them.

Thus, the "Is it art?" question is totally unhelpful, since it presumes the existence of standards that are absolute, and it is irrelevant to present developments. With modern "painting-sculpture" the onus is partly on the viewer to discover the standards by which a work behaves. Standards, like everything else now, are relative; they often seem to have little to do with art as we know it but a lot with the object in front of us. Looking at art, as well as making it, has become more complex.

In retrospect, a large amount of what one saw last season could be categorized under headings not usually considered artistic:

Entertainment: Work, frequently wired for light and sound, that engages the attention and more or less sustains it pleasurably without deeper ambitions.

Journalism: Includes the many varieties of protest, satire, social comment, whether intended or unintended, frequently done in a way that ignores many of the rules of formal etiquette.

Research: The work as experiment in what occasionally appears to be a search for absolute artistic ideas. Often manifests itself as a type of purism investigating perception and the interaction of object and eye. As in all research, there is a large degree of specialization.

Hybrids: The result of various inbreedings between accepted or semi-accepted styles (Abstract Expressionism, Pop, Purism, etc.) resulting most often (but not always) in test-tube oddities.

In each of these categories there is a repeated curiosity about the distinctions between, and interchangeability of, reality and illusion, which seems a concomitant to the transgression of art's accepted boundaries and conventions.

In a first step to establishing new standards, work within these categories can be judged as good or bad performance, if not as good or bad art. The good work challenges the critic and sends him looking for new yardsticks. In looking for these yardsticks there is an unfortunate willingness among some critics to take dictation from the artist's expressed aim, instead of going first to the artist's work, which seems to me the proper beginning.

Obviously, then, there is a new freedom from old conventions, a new attempt to extend the province of art, to redefine the relationship between life and art and to bring them closer together. Admirable though this may be, most of the results at present (though one may accept them with sympathy, at times with admiration, and always with a certain permissiveness for the farthest of far-out developments) are self-limited by the postulates on which they appear to base themselves.

But the present chaos of standards and styles is far from depressing if one interprets it as an expression of a new necessity to eliminate the conventional barriers between the arts for the purpose of creating a composite art that will relate to society in a new and unique way. Watching the new manifestations that appear to destroy all that we understand by art, we may be witnessing, without recognizing it, what we have long been waiting for—the beginning of a new, pliable, and flexible mode of expression suitable to our fluid and complex society. Should this be so, art, currently without standards and criteria but in search of new ones, may in the future be capable of injecting some meaning into life, because it has found some meaning in it.

July 1963
The New York Times

Art and Freedom—the Crisis of Style

A GREAT VICTORY for twentieth-century art was the achievement of freedom. Lately, it has begun to look like a defeat. Freedom, a necessity when fought for, has tended to become a license to produce a commodity.

When won by the pioneers at the start of the century, freedom meant "freedom from"—from morality, from society, from debasing realism and limiting humanism. At that stage art had the excitement and intoxication that is the first result of any acutely desired freedom newly won.

But for about the last twenty years, art, having exhausted the idea of freedom as a value in itself, has been finding it more and more of an embarrassment. In that time Abstract Expressionism fought a valiant battle to make total freedom meaningful. Lately there are signs that the artist is looking for a point of contact with his surroundings—social, physical, and philosophical—in a way he has not done before.

Some artists seem to be realizing instinctively that freedom is not an absolute thing, but only meaningful when related to something else. The trouble is finding the "something else" when imprisoned by the results of more than fifty years of total freedom. The really avant-garde artist today is investigating what philosophy formed conclusions about a hundred years ago—how to make freedom meaningful by relating it to something other than itself.

The results of freedom have left the contemporary artist in a position of confusion and anxiety. Like anyone who wants to make a contribution in this age of self-consciousness, he must know the score—what already has been done. As Harold Rosenberg pointed out, he will have no trouble finding out.

Reproductions open all past worlds to him, making him familiar with everything from Ur on. He is conversant with the forms of various historical arts, usually without much understanding of what produced them—a type of education encouraged in art history departments since "style" became the most important word in art.

He is also aware of everything in the contemporary art world the moment it happens. Magazines acquaint him with the latest thing from Tokyo to Rome. His freedom of choice is paralyzing. Eventually, in the usual course of events, he finds something for himself in the available library of styles that will enable him to cope with the problems of art as he sees them. From past and present, and presumably from himself, he forces that modern signature of originality—the "individual style." This "individual style," once it is achieved, is apparently the justification of freedom. Once a style is formed, the artist isn't allowed, by our present standards, to transgress it. There is little sympathy for the man who uses a few styles, or who says different things in different ways. A style is grooved allowing a logical progression, with the critic leapfrogging after the artist, cataloguing the course. Modern art has elevated style, like freedom, to an absolute value.

Deprived of any responsibility except the pursuit of style, most modern artists are really in search of a passable "original" eclecticism. Perhaps this is why most modern art, in one's moments of doubt, seems to take place in a huge vacuum with extraordinary chains of styles mirroring each other into some eclectic infinity. In complete freedom, style is the cage the artist has fashioned for himself. It is a discipline drawn from art, not from the conflict of art with life, and it seems increasingly arid.

Thus the main result of meaningless freedom is that it has translated itself into a crisis of style. Art develops from art, ignoring life; and a number of perfected styles are made available to bear content (abstract or literary) that they entomb. (At the galleries one can spot the "style" exhibition from the doorway—a selected style immuring its content to produce what is totally lifeless.)

In this regard style as an end in itself is the perfection of means without an end—reminding one of Einstein's statement that perfection of means and confusion of ends are typical of our society. Abstract Expressionism got around this brilliantly for a while by proving that means and end can be one, an excitingly existential affirmation of meaning.

The deification of style in modern art fostered the development of wars of attrition between stylistic coteries, each affirming the exclusive value of its own style—a conflict with remarkable similarities to the controversies of medieval schoolmen splitting scholastic hairs. Both were unrelated to life.

Because it is unrelated to life, most modern art in the galleries has substituted a motif for a theme. Any genuine invention, such as Abstract Expressionism, seems to go in the direction of art rather than life, toward academism rather than toward meaningful transformation. In the case of Abstract Expressionism, its initial vital energy was rapidly insulated from life by debased styles.

A vast dying area of modern art, then, has style but no theme. Themes have apparently been found either too big (mass atrocity) or too small (the personal lyric impulse). After about forty years of splendid freedom, followed by around twenty years of mostly meaningless freedom, art, to judge from some current developments, seems to be moving toward a theme. The theme seems to be an attempt to establish a positive relationship between the artist and his environment.

This is, of course, a great theme. All of us face the problem of preserving our individuality in a mass society without abdicating from society. As society has become more complex, increased responsibility toward each other has been forced on us, along with the realization that real freedom is associated with responsibility.

Thus the artist, finding total freedom from society its own kind of trap, is discovering a responsibility to himself to relate his work to his society. This is distinctly not to say he has a responsibility to the society, for that would be but a short-cut to social realism and the abuses that political idealism has perpetrated on the artist in the name of freedom.

If one is reading the signs right, the artist, having enjoyed the anarchy of total freedom from any responsibility to society, is now turning his attention toward a new definition of freedom within the framework of society. If this is so, art is about to tackle one of the major problems of living in this century.

July 1963
The New York Times

Color and a New Abstraction

COLOR, in its nature and effects, has been one of those endlessly productive mysteries—like electricity. There are signs (plenty of them at this stage) that a new type of abstraction based on color is hitting the galleries, an abstraction adding to investigations begun in the seventeenth century and continued ever since, concerning questions of reality and illusion, and of color as sensation, as light, and as space. Any understanding of the new abstraction must abandon the idea of color as a merely decorative adjunct to a picture, or even as a direct emotive stimulus. A color must be regarded as a structural unit, a spatial unit, or a unit of light or direct sensation, with its own capacity to react aggressively against another color. It may even have the capacity for motion. Colors played against one another may seem to leap forward, to recede, to jostle one another, as they compete for the eye's attention. At the edges or borders where colors meet there is a great deal of visual activity, forcing the eye to see more colors than are, in fact, really there.

Effects are produced through an exact knowledge of the eye's tolerance and limits, which are sometimes purposely transgressed. Indeed, some of the diagrams from Chevreul's classic book on color, *The Laws of Contrast of Colour and their Application to the Arts* (1839), now look like avant-garde paintings. The tension of these new paintings seems to be due mainly to the contrast of complementary colors at the same value or intensity. As simplicity of design is necessary in producing the urgent color effects, there is an emphasis on simple motifs—squares, chevrons, circles, linear bands. Astonishingly complex and ambiguous effects are produced by simple means.

Within this framework (which includes science, philosophy, and psychology) the current developments take on a meaning that emancipates them from the vacuum in which much modern art exists. Through color, the new images intuitively investigate such acutely modern obsessions as change and action.

The main quality of this more or less new abstraction (of which Morris Louis, because of his early death and the violently strait-jacketed pillars of color in his last works, has been elected prophet) is its abrupt immediacy. The image is thrust against the eye in manners ranging from the aggressively tender to the downright brutal. The eye is not free to wander, to select or reject, but is instantly forced to complete perceptions that are purposely made unstable and ambiguous.

In this new mode of abstraction the picture becomes both a stimulus and a screen on which the eye projects the changes taking place in it. The interaction of painting and observer is forced and the eye is kept in a state of crisis from moment to moment. In Abstract Expressionism the action was *on* the canvas. In the new abstraction, the action is *in* the onlooker's eye.

This new abstraction, or screen painting, as one might call it, has no program and is more a coincidence of painters than a movement. It can, however, point to a pretty impressive ancestry, especially since past parentage has become so important in legitimizing the present. A reasonable family tree might include Cézanne and Bonnard and Vuillard, Matisse, such para-Abstract Expressionist phenomena as Newman and Rothko, and some of Stuart Davis' snapping, staccato color contrasts. Any genealogy would also have to include that geometric Hamlet of modern abstraction, Josef Albers.

As practiced, the new abstraction has a wide range of activity, from art to anti-art, from the shockingly aggressive to the expressive, from impersonal mechanical precision to more or less obvious hand-painting. It runs from the brilliant, brutal, and blank bombardments of Larry Poons to the Bonnard-like curtains of Robert Natkin, from the single targets of Kenneth Noland to Thomas Downing's concentric bubbles, from the hard eclipses of Alexander Liberman to the eye-rubbing rinds of Jules Olitski. It includes such artists as Gene Davis, John Kacere, Edward Avedisian, the new Raymond Parker, possibly the recent Richard Barringer, occasionally David Simpson. All force the eye to attention through color. The best of them keep attention by switching the eye through multiple perceptions, through multiple actions.

At a certain stage some of this work does as much, or more, through the motif as through the color. Richard Anuszkiewicz's dazzingly multiplied motifs engage the eye through pattern and repetition, through warped perspectives and astigmatic effects that have a cousinship to experimental optical diagrams and charts. In fact, this brings us into the other great division of modern abstraction compelling the eye. One could call it chart painting—seen in its purity, without color, in the work of someone like Henry Pearson. Both of these optical modes have been turned to use in advertising design for years, and in Pop art recently. And their fundamental vocabulary has been in every psychology textbook for more than half a century.

Perhaps the direction to take in searching for meaing in the new art is to contemplate what it actually presents. Through limitation of means it establishes precision in ambiguity. That ambiguity, forcing the viewer's attention, makes him an active participant in a pictorial event. From this he gains a measure of individual identity depending on *his* sensations. New active relationships are developed between picture and observer, object and subject, means and end. The new art is factually objective, and yet as individual as the person who looks at it.

For the artist and viewer, individual freedom is made possible and meaningful within a strictly chosen and easily communicable discipline. Whatever one thinks about the larger social implications of this, one thing is certain. The new abstraction is important.

January 1964
The New York Times

Art Versus Feeling

I SUPPOSE YOU COULD call it a trend. It's more a new attitude than anything else—a deadpan, anti-feeling response to the problems of art and life manifested in what could be called, in a flourish of phrase-coining, the new nihilism within the new abstraction—the new abstraction being the "Optical" art splitting the eyes of gallery-goers all over town.

The new nihilism can best be defined in relation to something so opposite to it (Abstract Expressionism) that it could be patly construed as a reaction to that movement. Abstract Expressionism was a quest for identity through the motif that unlocked the self. In its emphasis on spontaneity and freedom, on action in an absolutely relative microcosm, Abstract Expressionism was a kind of self-portrait, a temporary existential solution to the problems of identity in a social vacuum. Its successes could be looked on as portraits of the self in crisis of conscience amidst the terrors of choice.

The new nihilism is first of all a total abnegation of the self. Brushstroke, the signature of self, is eliminated in favor of a smooth, anonymous finish. It is anti-spontaneous, its motifs logical, measurable, reproducible. Its logic, as in a Larry Poons or a Frank Stella, is used not to make a statement but to lead to a nonstatement, a nonrevelation that becomes the content of the picture. The new nihilism is brilliantly, and purposely, obtuse.

Identity and the self are ignored as, presumably, unimportant. Attention is caught by hooking the eye on its own reflexes. Poons, for instance, seems to concentrate on the excitation of the eye alone, and any subsequent expectation of meaning is ruthlessly frustrated.

This concentration on the eye, and the strict deprivation of the mind behind it, are curiously fascinating aspects of this art. Its anti-romantic, anti-emotional bias leads to disengagement, to noncommitment—a total reversal of Abstract Expressionism's emphasis on "engagement" and "commitment" as magic words. The only point of possible contact is that both movements respond to the same existential situation—one takes (or took) action; the other does not, and is content, with precise logic, to underline its absurdity.

The new nihilism marks the arrival of a new generation, a cool hip generation that has gone beyond *Angst* to indifference. Take for instance, the Bomb. To the generation born in the twenties, trying to cope with what could not be felt, it produced an agony of feeling. To some of the generation now in its mid-twenties, it is simply nothing to feel about. Feeling and emotion, judging by the new art, have been abandoned as methods of coping with the unfeelable and unrealizable problems that kept most of us in a state of acute, formless anxiety for years—the Bomb or the atrocities of the social machine grinding down individuality and feeling. Thus, as a method of coping, feeling just won't do—as evidenced by the almost total lack of moral outrage (which usually leads to expressionism) in the new generation of artists.

The response of the new nihilists to art and life is partly a defense reaction (to prevent hurt), possibly a hip post-Rimbaud attempt to dissociate sensation and emotion, and certainly an abandonment of emotion as a solution to problems that emotion can't begin to solve. In this it is totally practical in an amoral way—for emotional responses usually presuppose moral absolutes. The new nihilism forces us to realize that right and wrong are not absolutes, that some of our largest problems are most likely to be solved not as moral issues but as social and/or political issues—a terrifying sort of maturity in what is, on purpose, an unemotional art.

This neutrality of emotion and this annihilation of the self lead naturally to the largest implication of the new nihilism—expressed deadpan by a leading Pop artist (much of the same anti-emotional, anonymous bias can be found in Pop) when he said simply, "I wish I were a machine." This is much more than just funny.

The artist as mass-produced object producing objects in turn is a nightmare that has been felt (and satirized; remember Grandville?) ever since industrialization came in. The loss of identity has always been feared. Now the loss of identity is welcomed. Apparently the future disposition of such old antagonisms as romantic versus classic may be anonymity versus individuality, subject versus object.

The new nihilists may be the pioneers of a machinelike anonymous art in which personality, paramount since the Renaissance, disappears in the work. This removal of the self makes possible the remarriage of the artist and society in a modern context. Which opens up a host of new possibilities—and problems.

February 1964
The New York Times

A New Union of Art and Life

"NATURE AND ART," said Picasso in 1923, "being two different things, cannot be the same thing." That seems very dated now, even to the use of "nature," a word more at home in the preceding century than in this one.

Picasso's statement summarized a distinction vital to the evolution of an art breaking free from nature into what Lionello Venturi used to call its "autonomy"—art as a self-sufficient entity surviving through its inner formal relationships alone. But ideas remain vital only as long as they are useful, and Picasso's statement—basic to art since Cubism—isn't very useful any more. Now we are frequently surrounded by art that transgresses Picasso's distinction between art and nature, making the critic's distinction between form and content more or less impractical too.

The new era can be conveniently dated by another artist's statement, Robert Rauschenberg's marvelously provocative "Painting relates to both art and life. Neither can be made. (I try to act in the gap between the two.)" He said that in 1959, substituting for "nature" (a body separate from the observer) the word "life"—a process turning the observer into a participant. The implications of this switch are pointed up by some brilliant recent shows—George Segal's, Marisol's, perhaps Tom Wesselmann's, and what one remembers of Edward Kienholz's work imported from the West Coast.

All of them incorporate objects from daily life in constructions, tableaux, and environments—attaching them physically and psychologically to areas of painting and sculpture. Segal's white plaster figures (cast from life) sprawl beside a real Coke machine, sit dumbly on real bus seats, shave plaster legs in a real tiled bathroom. Marisol shuffles reality and illusion in a dislocating interplay between objects (shoes, musical instruments, a perambulator) and their constructed simulacra. Wesselmann recently stretched the tension between art and the object (or brute fact) as far as possible by painting a high-art nude in a bath with a real shower curtain, surrounded by a real door and clothes hamper.

Art and life (the daily object and the painted or worked object) are brought into a new equilibrium extending both into a twilight zone where each partakes of the other and only gains meaning in the presence of the other.

The most obvious fact about the undoubted success of these works is that the "art" component and the untransformed object are presented with an utter aplomb that becomes in itself an adhesive force holding them together. The deadpan brings the "art" into alignment with the dumb neutrality of real objects. Art and brute fact seesaw into a relationship with far-reaching implications—implications ignored when the invasion of art by the fact, by real life, is taken as a degeneration of art (which it can be, depending on the artist) or a fatal lack of transformation (a doubtful criterion, one has to admit now).

The use of the raw object naturally draws attention to its

history—from Cubist collage, through Duchamp's and Ernst's ready-mades, to Jasper Johns's ambiguous presentations of illusion as reality (cast beer cans, cast light bulbs). At this stage, such earlier adventures look like acute testings of the standards of art, or acts of discovery now being put to work. In an era that made art synonymous with transformation, they raised problems never solved—until now.

For suddenly one discovers that these new artists solve the question of transformation by showing that it isn't a question at all—it depends on older criteria to which they no longer subscribe. Transformation as a concept has given way to the idea of relationships as a criterion—the tensions established between "art" and raw objects, which are forced into an interaction by the participation of the observer. Take one of Segal's figures away from its environment and the environment relapses into brute fact. In the presence of the figure, the environment aspires to art, just as the plaster figure aspires to life, and the viewer is the crossroads through which this traffic takes place. The vital relationship is no longer the old idea of formal interaction on a canvas, but a balance between art and the brute fact mediated by the observer.

The natural extension of this "art plus life" construction into everyday space, the space we occupy in living, breaks down the "otherness" of art into a new fusion that may well contribute to the art of the future. It may have large implications of architecture, since this new art, like a building, is only meaningful when lived in. As in the new abstraction, art and observer depend on each other for their effects.

The best of this new work, trafficking in the gap between art and life, leads (especially in Segal's ordinary tableaux) to a new self-awareness, and a new questioning of self-identity. The constant movement of "reality" from the object to the "art" through the viewer is a confusing experience that eventually forces one to relinquish the idea of "reality" as a stable fact. The breakdown of the barrier between art and observer, between object and subject, forces us to locate "reality" (if the word still means anything) in the fluid shifts in and out of a field of relationships to which we contribute, and in which we are a changing factor—a system philosophy has long ago adopted in favor of the outdated notion of "reality" as a stable, knowable thing.

The essence of this new "reality" implied by such art as Segal's is that it is practical, livable in—the direct opposite of the "reality" of unseen forces that powered art into symbols for everything from the atom to astronomy. Its unstable location makes it part of what we may expect from art in the future, an art in formation now.

March 1964
The New York Times

The Rise of Art Below the Waist

THE SAVAGE, the raw, and the pornographic have become hip. There was a time (from Giorgione to Renoir) when sensuality was sublimated into the accepted forms of desire by artistic good manners. This is now hopelessly square. During the past few seasons there have been unending demonstrations of the clinical deglamorization of sex ("How frank you can be"), and the handling of pornography in an utterly deadpan way ("How cool you can be"). Perversion, obscenity, and just plain smut are now noteworthy on the art scene. From Francis Bacon to Pop, the trend to extend art's subject matter to the unmentionable has become a preoccupation. Whether it is a healthy or unhealthy one depends on your standards. But most artists I know seem to be engaged in some private sexual adventure on canvas.

In this, of course, art is catching up with movies, poetry, drama, and the novel, which have been over the same ground long ago with fairly clinical thoroughness, in the process both defining and obscuring the location of that troublesome zone in which art becomes pornography and vice versa. Recently I saw a brilliant new Pop movie by Raymond Saroff called *The Real Thing* that purposely switched from one side of that zone to the other in a dazzling opening. Commercialized sex, selling everything from vacations to beer, was interrupted by the exertions of a rather winsome couple in a pornographic movie, thus making a savage counterpoint between reality and illusion—and once more raising the question of whether pornography remains pornography when it is used to contribute to an artistic statement. Whether or not an "artistic statement" has been made is a problem that leads straight out on that well-worn route to the aesthetic and legal wilderness.

Anything goes. In 1963, Edward Kienholz set up a bordello, modeled on a real one near Las Vegas, in the Iolas Gallery in New York, complete with whore—not just painted à la Lautrec, but in 3-D, like an environment. The same artist—one of the liveliest around—already has contributed a classic to the artistic-sexual scene: a bare, bulb-lit bedstead set up with accouterments and called "The Illegal Operation." Most of this genitally fixated art, however, is less resourceful, contenting itself with sexual public relations—from Madison Avenue advertising copy right through to pure pornography. In either case, the public doesn't seem to mind.

We have come a long way from the sort of censorship that closed D. H. Lawrence's London show in 1923 because he painted pubic hair on his nudes. One of the odd things about the "breakthrough" in pornography is that nobody is upset by it. Which means that either sex or art has become so unimportant that neither any longer gets people where they live. With *Fanny Hill* receiving testimonials from clergymen, straight sex doesn't seem to have any shock value left.

Neither does perversion. At the Guggenheim Museum in the fall of 1963, Francis Bacon's canvas of homosexuals copulating in some bizarre psychological ambience telescoping assault and desire—one of the most daring pictures in the history of "subject" in art—was passed over with the same devoted inattention given a Mondrian. The neuralgic sensibility and lurid tabloid subject matter, although new in art, were happily accepted by people who can still be upset, however slightly, by Burroughs' *Naked Lunch* and Rechy's *City of Night*. Nothing more acutely illustrates the inability of art to shock a public that short-circuits every artistic experience by complete acceptance, on the assumption that because it is "art" it has nothing to do with anything halfway important—outside a gallery, that is.

There is barely a hundred years' distance between Bacon's frank presentation of what often looks like sex murder and Hiram Powers' chaste "Greek Slave," clothed in its nudity like some modesty vest, but still considered a shocker in its own time. But it leads to contemplation of the awesome light-years between the conventions within which the human spirit can, apparently, function. Pornography, like beauty or any other form of prejudice, is in the eye of the beholder. Each generation, as we well know, attaches its own taboos that often appear ludicrous to the next. Victorian pornography (in photographs especially) now looks like Great-aunt Millie who somehow got undressed by mistake. Nothing dates so quickly as pornography with its implied sexual attitudes, and I suppose this puts some perspective on what is taking place now in art. What is currently brutal, or wilfully perverted, or totally frank, may appear charmingly "period" in the future.

Some of the art one sees now is certainly sexy or cheeky in ways that tie up easily with traditions of the naughty. Ben Johnson's jelliform nudes, undressed up to but not including their hats, are heirs to some phylogenetic cross between Modigliani and Marie Laurencin—and students who write papers on such things are probably connecting him to Boucher.

Harold Stevenson, at the Feigen Gallery in Manhattan, used essentially standard means to produce a nude environment. Nudity is something you think of stripping down to, but Stevenson made it something you walked into. He performed this alchemy by painting a huge, conventional nude reclining across three walls, turning the corners strategically with a phallus the size of a bicycle pump.

One could go on listing the updating of conventional styles in sex, anatomy, and pornography, without much profit. As a footnote to that decision, the most mature conventional use of genitalia I have seen was in Rico Lebrun's illustrations for Brecht's *Threepenny Novel*. His lumbering microcephalic creatures circled each other impotently, their genitals expressing emotions more usually read in faces—puzzlement, anguish, despair, lust, eagerness, with occasional gleams and spasms of happiness. The actual faces were shrunken or blankly brutal. It was done with an expressive seriousness a long way from the simple pleasures of mere exposure—an unsophisticated end to which some artists apply themselves with the most sophisticated of means.

Pornographic effectiveness apparently depends a great deal on fetishistic fixations on articles of clothing that partially conceal, suggest, and stimulate more than unadulterated nakedness—which can, as anyone who has leafed through a nudist magazine knows, be pretty unpornographic. A notebook could be filled with what turns up in and on current paintings—from underwear (bras, panties, girdles, often find a permanent home in collages in a sexual and aesthetic double play) to Freudian symbols, most commonly that old reliable, the glove.

The fetishistic emphasis is strong in such paintings as Richard Lindner's, whose strapping women are frequently bound up in obese parcels with elasticized, sinister underwear. Not too long ago, a Pop show by Copley (again at Iolas) provocatively ravaged one of these panty-and-bra stores for the grotesquely exaggerated underwear that makes women look like clowns, except to someone in the heights of an undiscriminating passion.

The commercial exploitation of garment fetishism has destroyed excitement by just such ludicrous exaggeration. Seymour Krim blasted off against this devaluation of underwear as sexual coinage in a marvelous piece called "The Magical Underwear Party (with Detachable Garters)":

From TV newspaper shopwindow subway—lifesize—poster into the snatch-blazing eye of the sly pornographic fantasying boy-sexed American man comes the new bold march of bras panties disembodied girdles and the whole secret universe of underwear bliss that once was the petticoated mystery of woman! As cold blushless ultra-realistic merchandising of the fetishistic holy garments of female becomes an avalanche—as the bras dance coyly across TV screen and the panty-girdles wiggle brashly between reels of Late Movie and the dark dirty-magazine caves of throat-drying sexscent are ripped open in frankness of Playtex-Longline-Bali-Bandeau-by-Exquisite Form—U.S. man and woman both squirm and flush in the vise of historical change!

Mass sex, coming down the commercial supply route like an avalanche, was diverted into art by way of Pop a year or two after this essay was written in 1959. It is surprising that it had to wait so long—witness the fact that Beat poetry, its counterpart, had swallowed up the world years before with an appetite far in excess of its capacity to digest. The reason for the lag was probably the total success of Abstract Expressionism as a style, a fashion and a way of life. It excluded anything that disturbed what its best critic called "the tension of the painter's lonely and perilous balance on the rim of absurdity. . . . " It disappeared (in America, art styles don't just transform into something else—they are wiped out of existence by the succeeding style), when it was destroyed by the corrupt social forces it had momentarily held at bay. Which explains, by and large, why Abstract Expressionists haven't a good word to say for Pop, which they identify with these forces, since Pop uses their packaged products. At that point, around 1961, while Abstract Expressionism was suffering the malaise of total misunderstanding and total success, very few people had any idea that Mass Man was waiting in the wings with an erection, ready to step onstage.

So was a new kind of artist—the hipster, the cool cat who had already run his course in poetry and the novel. It took a while for critics (including this one) to realize that his deadpan presentation of largely untransformed reality was just that—deadpan, without any implied social comment, a disinterested presentation (instead of a re-presentation) of life, very often in the raw.

When Willem de Kooning, in the middle of his "Woman" series in the fifties, produced one creature (devastated by a post-Cubist wrenching of planes, wearing a bland, rubber-lipped mouth clipped from a magazine), who later picked up the name "Marilyn," he little knew he was providing an ancestor figure for the art of the sixties. The brief Marilyn cult died out fairly quickly, but the sexual orientation of much Pop art did not. Sex as a packaged product, usable, disposable, always new, insulated from the rest of life by its exclusive focus, is too integral a part of the environment. It also seems to fascinate artists who want to show how cool they can be by passing on potentially explosive material without any emotion at all.

Recently you could have seen the following examples on public display: Rosalyn Drexler's small, thickly painted pinups modeled on the crude four-color photographs featured by pornography emporiums; William Kent's prints incorporating line drawings of sexual positions taken from some elementary sexual primer; Andy Warhol's serialized bare bosoms stenciled onto a canvas and visible only under ultraviolet light.

All these manifestations of the new age were visible at something called "The First International Girlie Show" at the Pace Gallery in January 1964. The opening was embellished by three cuties wearing scanties and nunlike expressions of resignation while serving pink champagne—which still didn't help the pictures. Not represented were a persistent and embarrassing trio, Sam Goodman, Boris Lurie, and Stanley Fisher, who for years have been using the most obscene pinups available as collage material in obvious social commentaries; e.g., a sexy nude next to grisly photographs of gas-chamber victims piled up in insectlike walls.

The best Pop art puts into glaring focus whole segments of life— the pornographer's twilight zones, the arcades where the strippers jerkily do it again and again every time the nickel drops, the novelty stores, the shady movie houses, the small ads at the backs of magazines, all the dolorous acreage of how-to-do-it manuals anxious to help the American male (and female, I suppose) to achieve, through their dedicated impersonal service, the Great Personalized Orgasm. In this light, sexually fixated Pop is a cruelly heedless concentration of the dilemmas of Mass Man—hoping and hetero-sexual, bogged down in his pornography substitutes (whose temples are the no-touch Playboy Clubs), devoured by his frigid wife, aging into ulcers and heart attacks, reading up on "How to Achieve Satisfying Orgasm" and "How to Achieve Happiness," which he feels sure are directly connected. Mass Man is the only figure that can support tragedy, now that individuals are too unimportant. Pop art focuses on the iconography of his Passion as it looms from billboards, flashes from the TV screen, head full of headache-producing hammers, stomach dripping with great pools of acid, hemorrhoids eager to shrink without surgery.

The cool impersonal attitude of Pop art has, of course, the great advantage that it opens up all possible experience with the assurance of being able to handle it—including the bleak frontiers of the coldest and most unconventional passion or perversion. In the latest art, sex seems to have been depersonalized by curiosity. It is a curiosity more disinterested than clinical, as if sex were not so much something *between* two people with which they communicate as it is something apart from them which they examine, pass with mild curiosity from one to the other, while they both approach a more neuter gender by each taking on the characteristics of the other— the boy more passive, the girl more the hunter.

In art now, as in life, the conventions that used to determine what was "normal" in sexual mores have expanded to include so much, that sex, for all the emphasis on it, seems strangely unimportant.

June 1964
Show

Mapping Our Camp Sites

THE INTELLECTUAL'S BUBBLE-GUM CARDS have been switched and now one Andrews Sister can get you two Ubu Rois. The art of Margaret Dumont and the audience rapport of Lili St. Cyr have become matters of intellectual status. Jerry Lewis' atavistic recipes for instant madness are currently being established as a subject for serious study. The popular arts have become—popular. Or, more truly, intellectually fashionable.

So now the object of popular culture, whether it be a Bette Davis movie, a comic strip, or a hot dog, is surrounded by attitudes that establish a pecking order against the object itself, a spectrum running from brute acceptance to an elaborate shuffling of self-conscious attitudes. It's a pity these attitudes were given a name— Camp—and are thus constantly defused by an abstract concept, an easy catch phrase, like the "cool" of a few years ago.

The rise of this self-consciousness is accompanied by the phenomenon of people establishing intellectual and often social status by their attitudes towards popular culture. In the classless society the classes are all in the mind. A widespread and genuine interest in the popular arts of past and present has, in the past few years, been invaded by fashion and by an intellectual elite whose approach is naturally exclusive. At the same time the avant-garde in the novel, theater and visual arts is being publicized and popularized. Popular

221

arts being made exclusive; exclusive arts being popularized—it makes a nice switch.

Into all this buzz and tickle, *The Popular Arts** heaves from England, like a rescue ship. It comes from a tradition that hasn't had much fashionable attention—that of responsible and discriminating inquiry into the nature of popular culture, an inquiry that goes as far back as Matthew Arnold's *Culture and Anarchy* and numbers Richard Hoggart's *On the Uses of Literacy* among its more recent classics. It is a tradition generally free of the two moralities the popular arts have been subjected to: the morality of indignation, the everything's-going-to-the-dogs reaction, and the more insidious aesthetic morality, the idea that there are purities in the popular arts that may be distilled from their contaminated surroundings. Frankly educational—it is directed to teachers—this book demands not just improvement in the mass media (practically speaking, a pretty futile kind of idealism) but discrimination in the response of the audience.

If it were not so outstandingly sensible, *The Popular Arts* would be a square book on how to be hip—square because it is so deadly serious about developing one's critical abilities in the midst of mass culture, a way of *living* in such a culture without rejecting it; in other words, how to inherit the twentieth century as well as live in it. "The struggle between what is worthwhile and what is shoddy and debased is not a struggle *against* the modern forms of communication, but a conflict *within* these media. . . . This book attempts to develop a critical method for handling these problems of value and evaluation in the media."

The authors' immediate aim is the enlightened introduction of the popular arts into the school curriculum in order to evolve values for practical living and to break down the insulation of most present-day academic teaching. The book proceeds from definitions of popular culture to individual themes and examples (among them

* *The Popular Arts*, by Stuart Hall and Paddy Whannel.

Billie Holiday, Mickey Spillane, the British TV serial "Coronation Street," Fleet Street's *Daily Mirror*), to a brief look at the institutions controlling communications (here mainly the film industry), then to a sampling of pros and cons in the literature of mass culture, and finally to suggestions for study. The tone is cool and grave, precise targets are sighted, and the few generalizations are wary— perhaps too wary.

One constantly implied generalization of *The Popular Arts* could have been made more explicit: the popular arts should not be spoken of, or studied, or criticized without some knowledge of the context in which they operate. And this should be asserted despite the fact that "context" criticism has often been a fatal door through which critics have passed and never come back, slipping into the sociology of the mass media instead of criticism of the popular arts. The limits of the possible in the mass media are constantly undergoing definition by the machinery of the economic and social system. The popular arts are in this way the arts of free enterprise, the iconography of capitalism, and this context of production, distribution, and consumption, inseparable from popular art, is the proper framework for criticism. What is possible naturally defines what can be done.

It seems self-evident and simple. Yet every day turns up new misapplications of standards ending up with distressed opinions on why a horse is not a camel. Broadway's streamlined assembly line is attacked for not being the nursemaid of the American theater; TV is hit for good formula ("The Beverly Hillbillies") as well as for routine formula ("Gunsmoke"); *Rififi* is played down, while its clumsy satire, *Big Deal on Madonna Street*, is played up. When the idea of art enters, so does a whole system of false values (*Red Desert*, a beautiful disaster, was widely respected). When exclusive, or high, art and popular art mix, there is total confusion.

Because he exists within a context, the popular artist (unlike the exclusive artist who creates his audience by a process of conversion, aided increasingly, it must be said, through public relations) creates

223

within shared conventions and assumptions. From pop music to movies these conventions include a set of formulas. Here Hall and Whannel come in (as others are beginning to do) with their idea of *style* separating popular art (good) from mass art (bad)—" . . . the way the communication is made, and its internal and implied rhythms and emphasis . . . is the only way of rendering fully our response to the material and the values confirmed or neglected within it." It is within this sequence describing the machine that the critical questions take shape: Are the techniques and stereotypes infused with life—with feeling rather than counterfeit feeling? What is the nature of the feedback from audience to artist and how reliable are the methods of determining it? How are fashions initiated and tastes defined?

The mass media are not in themselves corrupt. It is simply that their functional use precedes their artistic use: their conventions are formed by business, not art. The struggle within a medium to break these conventions and to define itself as an art (e.g., *Citizen Kane*, *L'Avventura*) is a subtheme continually feeding into the mainstream. It is not a main theme. The conventions are extraordinarily tough and sometimes seem to have a charming morality of their own—witness the rapid failure of an attempt to manufacture "Pop Gospel" a few years back, and the success of Phil Spector's passionate invasion of a powerful pop music monopoly in the name of a new generation.

Now that popular culture has been assiduously farmed by artists and writers for the past five years, it has provided a huge amount of material once thought unusable (in one of Irvin Faust's stories, the real hero is a transistor radio), and new techniques (mostly derived from montage—movies now seem to be the mother of the arts, although one cynic thinks the TV commercial is). And commercial ideas of reproduction, disposability, and rapid exhaustion are translated into a belief in provisional values and temporary solutions. The contemporary moment comes first—and it may be all there is. (Take some object art like Richard Artschwager's furniture—its parody of degenerate Bauhaus modern is firmly bound to this moment. Or take Irvin Faust again: the language in *Roar, Lion, Roar* is so aggressively tied to its New York 1965 locus that it seems patois outside it, and will each year become more encysted in a time capsule.)

Attitudes as a way of coping have become so widespread that the hypothetical monster Mass Man is in danger of fading away altogether. Everyone is learning how to slip on a disguise or deadpan and "put on" anything that isn't with it—*i.e.*, that doesn't share the attitude that it's all a bit of a game in which you must out-attitudinize the other guy (which partly explains Tom Wolfe and *fin-de-siècle* modern).

One of the positive developments in the liaison of exclusive and popular art is the development of a sensibility that can scan a barrage of stimuli and select the input—a computerlike response enabling survival and action in situations of instability and change. To watch this sensibility being tested, one should have seen the public at the Museum of Modern Art's Op show, or the older members of the audience at the film version of *The Knack*.

Popular art is still too widely considered degenerate, trivial, or dishonest. It often is. Avant-garde art that traffics in it often is dishonest too, but presumably that is one of the reasons for having critics. Popular culture desperately needs critics capable of making distinctions, of analyzing and applying new attitudes as they occur. It's fine to talk of how the talkies ruined the pure art of Chaplin or how Disney has declined since Snow White opened her motion-picture rosebud mouth. The real commitment in criticism of popular culture is always right *now*, as are the invitation and challenge to live in it.

August 1965
Book Week

Looking at the Artist as Performer

IN THE PAST DECADE art, which used to fall into fairly well-defined categories of painting, sculpture, and graphics, has boiled over these boundaries and seems to have become at the same time another form of activity. Instead of being described as artists and sculptors, artists and sculptors now seem better defined in a category that cuts across these ancient distinctions—performer.

The artist as performer is nothing new—but its present emphasis is. As an idea it brings into focus much of the violent diversity and clamorous supermarketism of the "international scene," where the giant shows (São Paulo, Venice, Carnegie, though not the Kassel Dokumenta) look more and more like artistic Olympics with performers measured against criteria more athletic than aesthetic. But underneath the obvious abuses (which is where one always has to look nowadays) there is the hard fact that art is aspiring to some form of theater, and many of its greatest successes (and abuses) are best understood in terms of performing, as some kind of acting.

The theatrical parallel, of course, fits much European art like a glove. From Giotto on, one could make a case for much European painting as "tableau" art, and for the artist as stage director. The drama becomes quite overt with the theatrical devices of Caravaggio and the perfectly coached actors of Poussin—a theatricalism which, overcoming naturalism, ran rampant in the Baroque, frequently descended into triviality with rococo and survived as degenerated theater, sentimental storytelling, in the nineteenth.

The great abstract take-over at the beginning of this century that eradicated and purged obvious sentiment could, in this context, be judged not a revolution at all. It could be considered the disguise of drama in modern (i.e., abstract) dress. The actors become abstract elements in conflict, resolved in a final balance that was frequently designated "dynamic," and the word "tension" entered every

226

critic's vocabulary. (The most overused words of every critical era may very well be the truest index of that era's art, hidden behind the obvious.)

With the rise of formal criticism, every art-history student learned to identify the elements of this drama (color, form, line, mass, tone, etc.) and their area of action (space). The more avant-garde critics, taking a cue from science, discovered that a formal dialogue in space involved time, so there were learned discussions of time-space and the relationship of art and science in the twentieth century.

The artist at this stage became perhaps more choreographer than dramatist or stage director—and the critics described abstract events, freed, like a dancer, from gravity. These abstract dramatics had much of the diversity, the modes of action and inaction, of modern theater. Tellingly enough, some twentieth-century art movements shared a name with twentieth-century theatrical movements, e.g., Expressionism, Dada, and Surrealism. With the latter two the distinction between art and theater was frequently eliminated.

It was with Abstract Expressionism that critics first began consistently describing artists as "performers" (the derogatory converse was "decorator"), and grading them according to "performance." With the emphasis on "gesture" and "action" (with learned diagnoses of pressure, speed, almost muscle tone, made from the calligraphs), one began to get a double image of what was hailed as the single ultimate image in art: the picture, and behind it, the artist, like some gesticulating ghostly presence. The idea of the Abstract Expressionist as performer wasn't very profitable, since it tended to displace attention from the painting to the artist, under the illusion that it was fusing both.

The idea also ignored the irresolvable antithesis between painting and action, and the fundamental impossibility of making the painting become, instead of stand for, an act. (Perhaps one can say that art is not emotion, but skillfully counterfeited emotion.) Yet

227

without this tension of the impossible, Abstract Expressionism became academic. At its best it acted out, in art, dilemmas that it wasn't in the nature of art to support (here Pollock, Kline, and De Kooning before 1954 are the exemplars). Thus, while seemingly summarizing the course of modern art (and getting all hung up on scholastic analyses of form and space), Abstract Expressionism was destroying that tradition by using art for purposes beyond its capacity—a tendency sometimes directly recognizable as anarchic and anti-art.

The ambiguities inherent in Abstract Expressionism are dazzling —and confusing. No movement changes more, depending on how you look at it—in itself a recognition of its importance as a hinge on which art has turned—in the process dividing artists, critics, and dealers as nothing has in years.

If one is to look for the real aspect of performing in Abstract Expressionism, it is in the direct choreography of Jackson Pollock (which still can be witnessed in Hans Namuth's photographs and film), in whom the process of painting seemed continuous and uninterrupted, and in the habit of some of its best practitioners (such as Franz Kline) of improvising sketches, of which one was selected, blown up, and adapted. This latter habit is much more like acting in that it developed a method of giving an appearance of spontaneity by mimicking the original impulse and its closeness to life.

In this there were similarities of approach between Method acting, as practiced here, and Abstract Expressionism—in the conscious breakdown of discipline for the subtle discipline of risk, in the uses of accident, in the exploration of the self, and in the relation of artist and actor to what they are doing.

In Abstract Expressionism, acting something out with a refusal to accept the fixed borders of art for this purpose led to an agony of impasse that was "solved" by succeeding art—simply by avoiding the state of mind that produced the impasse and continuing the idea of acting in a much more practical, not necessarily better, way.

Naturally, Abstract Expressionism, with its creative self-dramatization (it had to be hurting to be good) despised this "solution"—or evasion, depending on which side of the fence you're on.

But the break is not as obvious as it appears, if you follow up the acting idea, which makes the antagonistic division between subject and abstraction unnecessary. Both the triumph of subject known as Pop and the manipulation of perception known as Optical art are antagonistic to almost everything Abstract Expressionism stood for, but they continue the idea of performance vigorously and unselfconsciously.

Both Pop and Optical art share a liking for high, saturated color with a capacity to engage and fatigue the retinal cells. Sometimes both move physically, play with light, and are good for just one performance—when you've seen them you've seen them—leading to the idea of disposability. But the main point is that, as with a book or a movie, you are frequently forced to wait while the works go through their paces, or while they put your eye through its paces. There is also the extension of recent art into the everyday space in which the viewer stands, something that can be traced to the vast size of Abstract Expressionist canvases, which forced a new physical relationship between art and viewer. More recent art produces situations and environments to which the observer has to relate and respond. And recently many artists have at some stage moved into overt performing media—movies, theater, even ballet.

In this post-Abstract Expressionist art the effects are often, when considered as performance, climaxless and repetitious—bringing one to the artistically vital area (both in theater and art) of monotony and boredom. In Optical art the abrupt cycle of "perception-breakdown-new perception" is such that it might be called boredom at a high level of interest. A type of primitive interest (because it is acute and involuntary) is sustained by the most sophisticated means.

This performance element comes in because Optical art, at its best, is a cleverly camouflaged virtuoso performance on the eye through its reflexes. Optical art has produced a repertory of stimuli which play on the eye's capacity to distinguish colors, forms, repetitions. The play is naturally as good and as bad as the artist conducting it. The idea of the eye as instrument is a very old one, but the vital desire to test that instrument through all its possibilities is new. In Optical art the artist makes the viewer perform for his own (the viewer's) benefit, to "screen" his own responses. The observer unconsciously becomes an actor before the picture from which the artist has eliminated himself.

With Pop the performing aspect is frequently in the acting out of a single idea in different ways. Pop is fundamentally an art of ideas, and with an idea the problem is to work it out successfully. The old question of means and end, which Abstract Expressionism fused, arises again.

In Pop the end, in a peculiarly modern inversion, serves the means. The idea is only as good as the way in which it is carried through. Enlarging a plate and cutlery to elephantine proportions may be a good idea. But unless the means have distinction, as they have with Alex Hay, for instance, the idea turns into a gimmick.

Jim Dine and Claes Oldenburg are good examples of the idea man as performer. Dine hit on a good idea of a bathroom with toothbrush, mirror, and glass set up so as to be suitable only for an elasticized giant. Then he did what looked like a hurried (and indifferent) show based on this idea. Then he got another idea (the huge palettes in the Jewish Museum's black-and-white show) and came through. It was much like watching an actor in a bad show who switched into a new idea and was a hit. Similarly, Claes Oldenburg never did anything to me with his painted-food idea, but his soft typewriters and huge light fixtures are tiptop performances. Before, when artists went bad they usually stayed bad. Pop men are up and down, just as on Broadway.

Sometimes one basic idea can be adapted to many successful performances—the idea of word games, of anonymity, of size, of art as an inert object, etc. Most of these ideas throw some sort of performing strain on the spectator too. Ideas of size and anonymity put his self-image through various contortions to accommodate itself to the idea forced on it. In this Pop draws ideas from such areas as silent movies, fun fairs, and burlesque.

The performing idea is implicit in a lot of the most recent art (you can't call Pop and Optical art "new" any more). The idea of the artist as some sort of performer or stage director or actor or mime or virtuoso involves at the core a changed relationship between the artist and his work, and his work and the observer. Sometimes the artist seems to present his work of art as a kind of substitute actor (Kinetic art), sometimes he acts out ideas around the spectator (much Pop), sometimes he makes the spectator stand in his place and act out a set of sensations (Optical art). One might also speculate on the role of an audience "programmed" in a fashion that sets a boundary on its reactions. Here one moves into the area of artist and observer mimicking each other through stimulus and response, or "feed-in" and processing, to put it in the mechanical terms to which it seems to aspire.

If one follows the idea of the artist as performer to its logical conclusion one has standards of judgment that seem applicable to recent art. For one comes across all the uses and abuses of performance already more or less there in theatrical precedents.

There is, for instance, the hit light comedy (Leo Jensen); the comedy of blithe mindlessness with serious, almost sinister, undertones (Andy Warhol); melodrama (Rosalyn Drexler); pure entertainment (a host of names including some Op men); the avant-garde play (Marisol); the slice of life drama (George Segal). One could go on and on, mostly, of course, in the pop area. The question is: How good is the performance and how good are the ideas being acted out? The former standards of visual art apply only insofar as they contribute to the performance being good or not.

Thus, all the above modes of expression are totally admissible ways of practicing art, all cut across the idea of art as high art, which is apparently dying so hard. Art is anything the artist makes it—if he's good enough. If he wants it to be light entertainment or heavy drama, that's fine—just as long as he and we realize there's a difference in value between light entertainment and real drama.

August 1964
The New York Times

Boredom and the Amiable Android

THERE ARE innumerable ways of categorizing the art of the 1960s. One still hears most frequently of Op and Pop, the Tweedle-dum and Tweedledee of the cocktail-party circuit. More informed people can speak of "Ob"—for Object art—and when the Museum of Modern Art has its Kinetic show, "moving" art will be in there along with the others. Oppositions are also seen as categories—realism and abstraction, art of motion and art of rest, art of "process" and art of containment are among the oppositions set up to handle ideas and elaborate on the attitudes "behind" or in the art. Such oppositions cut across distinctions crudely, but they can have a certain temporary use. Perhaps one can at the moment add two categories—high-boredom and low-boredom art—to lead one into the elusive attitudes and subtle contradictions through which the art of the sixties is brought into being.

One can't suffer too long at the perceptual shocks, ripples and make-and-break currents of Optical art (a grab-bag term for at least three major lines of development) without realizing how domineeringly it involves the spectator. Similarly, Pop, when it uses "optical" color, partakes of this attack, urgently pushing its democratic images (though Pop has moved away from its heroic gastronomic stage of hamburgers and Coca-Cola in which anxiety seems to be smoothed under the iconography of "healthy" communal appetite. Environmentally, Pop has had a tendency to "match" the spectator's experience without attempting to "solve" it.) Few arts have been so persistent as Op and, occasionally, Pop, in drawing attention to themselves, and few have been so mute once attention is secured—leading, in turn, to an exhaustion of attention, a high-level boredom, like some of those technological miracles that demand wonder beyond the dutiful capacity to sustain it.

High-level boredom has a well-defined movie tradition of its own now in those attempts to redo the incessant kineticism of the silent screen with sound added, from *One, Two, Three* to *It's a Mad, Mad, Mad, Mad World* and now *Help.* The gimmickry used to sustain attention has been the subject of much analysis—both in art (long since wired for sound, light, movement and shock) and in movies (the classic sight gags updated) to which art often seems to aspire through what used to be called Happenings and now seems weakly categorizable as a modern form of nontheater to which a month was devoted in New York recently, featuring works by Oldenburg, Whitman, Dine, and others.

If high-boredom art depends for its effect on suddenly forcing attention and then exhausting it, low-boredom art doesn't force attention and, in fact, is easily ignored outside the self-conscious context of the gallery situation. It tends to fade into the environment with a modesty so extreme that it is hard not to read it as ostentatious. It is a kind of anonymous, featureless art whose existence seems to depend mainly on the fact that it is simply there, and has debts to pay for its existence to the de-symbolizing activity of Jasper Johns in his conversion of flags and targets into exquisite objects. Its forms seem less related to art than to some mundane but puzzling function. Some of it, like Richard Artschwager's, is based on the planned facelessness of contemporary furniture, and Claes Oldenburg produced a whole bedroom of such "furniture" in 1963 at the Janis Gallery, all artfully skewed into a display-case perspective.

Other work in this low-boredom object category has come from Donald Judd, Robert Morris, from a new young artist, Robert Smithson, and, in another aesthetic direction, from Lyman Kipp. All the work—like the best art of the mid-sixties—is notable for its rejection of the metaphorical tradition, the expression of one thing in terms of a second, which, through this displacement, illuminates the first. In Object art, which low-boredom art often is, the displacement is all. The object in some of Robert Morris' work can be of heroic scale, and the instinct is to relate to it as one does to many space-occupying functional objects (e.g., air-conditioning ducts)— physically clambering around it, psychologically turning it off. Here art has succeeded in mimicking man-made "nature" to an extent that parodies one tendency of Pop—the tendency to turn popular objects and environments off and on: now it's a delicatessen counter, now it's a great piece of Pop. This, of course, could be construed as a criticism of the Pop aesthete of the sixties, who now has the equipment (of attitudes) to see virtually anything as a work of found art. They are the successors to the "texturologists" of the fifties, who turned on to such found art as billboard collages, stained walls, rags; who again in turn are the successors to the Surrealist mineralogists of the thirties and forties who found "art" in natural configurations, stones, driftwood, etc., and who themselves reach back beyond Duchamp and Ernst to the nineteenth-century connoisseurs of the sentimental fragment (shells, hair) and beyond that again to the picturesque.

Another fact about mid-sixties art is that a new tendency, which appears to be hermetic, or limited to one particular statement, masks what is essentially a whole range of attitudes: and Object art ranges from a useless parody of function to a new purism—the object as the exact projection of an idea. Here one finds oneself shading into another area of great vitality in modern art—the serialization of "object" shapes into constructions that become environmental or architectural, such as those of Ronald Bladen. (Distantly related, insofar as they seem to offer an intermediate stage, are the individually meaningless fragments of George Sugarman's arbitrary progressions and David Weinrib's serialized plastic units. This aesthetic to some extent ties up with the dissociated coincidental events in Happenings. In a Jim Dine Happening, for instance, one group switches handkerchiefs, another eats and watches TV, another medicates plaster rags on an operating table, another saws metal tubing, another is the author in the midst of it all, another is his recorded voice. This is an entirely different tradition from Surrealist juxtaposition and association, which has been reactivated in the past year. It is a tradition of nonassociation of parts in the context of a continuing process, derived from de Kooning, and is, in fact, a remote translation of Abstract Expressionist process.)

Between boredom by exhaustion and boredom by indifference there is conceivably a stage where the sensational urgency of the former unites with the scrupulous formal clarity of the latter (the formal qualities of high-boredom art are hard to evaluate since the work is emphasized as irresistible stimulus more than anything else). At this intermediate stage, what turns up, paradoxically, is an art of the exquisite. A frequent color is that old "vulgar" de Kooning pink, now a Revlon shade of cosmetic camouflage. It can be seen in the work of some of the shaped-canvas artists—Charles Hinman, Richard Smith, Sven Lukin—which is part object and part painting, engineered into an intermediate existence for which no good name has yet been found. Exquisite color is also a property of painting whose optical dynamism has been scaled down to allow its sensuous and decorative qualities to predominate. Backing into this middle area, from this perspective, one can point to the work of Morris Louis and Kenneth Noland.

The terms high- and low-boredom art, arbitrary as they are, are useful in that they lead naturally to some of the main concerns of art in the sixties—to the ironies they conceal, to the techniques by which they are executed (Jackson Pollock's pioneering use of a "nonartistic" means, aluminum paint, has been succeeded by a host of others—plastics, chromium, spray-gun enamels, etc.), and to the "mimicking" of the machine, which in the last few years has constituted a new orthodoxy of unfreedom and freedom. Recently Wylie Sypher wrote: "The critical problems of our new art, and new science, are chance, indeterminacy, absence, and the illusions of space and time—being and nothingness. Far from being anarchy, the new painting and the new music intently study the emergence of form from the formless, of necessity from accident, of music from noise, of purpose from purposelessness, of art from the random. Essentially this is an art related to a computer-culture."

All but the last sentence could have been written in the fifties. Chance as a mode of freedom has been prejudiced ever since Rauschenberg painted two almost exactly similar Abstract Expressionist pictures. Now chance is simply a built-in variable to the most sophisticated—and literally most stupid—of machines, the computer. Its caricature is art as a computerized nonsymbolic object whose function is reduced to "thereness" in a world where people are objects too. Andy Warhol has become famous for his bright refusal to take on more responsibility than a machine, which leads to the fiction of an autolobotomized euphoria in which repetition and boredom are prime values. This perfect euphoria was perfectly expressed by Wyn Chamberlain in a remarkable exhibition of his friends, nude as Playmates, in happy beach-party groups.

Art simply becomes a function in a world of other more or less useful functions. Object art, for instance, becomes part of the art function. A gesture by Gerald Laing and Peter Phillips, two British artists, illustrates the object as fulfilling the "art-function." They attempted to define, through market research—canvassing dealers, critics, collectors—the nature of an all-purpose art object which could then be mass-produced. Laing was quoted as saying, "Why not apply industrial techniques to produce non-useful objects too?" A repertory of variables—of shape, size, color configuration, material, etc.—were provided. This constitutes a communal acceptance for art well below the alienation level.

Somewhat similarly, Optical art's perceptual attack forces acceptance at a level of psychophysiology. It becomes, in the extreme, an art substitute that keeps the brain circuits in a computerized tizzy, like a controlled hallucinogen. The involuntary nature of this response puts it within calling distance of Huxley's "soma." A recent movie illustration (turned, of course, into a brainwashing technique) was the highly inventive audio-visual environment in which the hero of *The Ipcress File* found himself. In this context, Optical art can be conceivably computerized, i.e., broken down into cybernetic "bits" and stated in electronic terms. This also brings one—through the door of Optical art—into the area of psychophysiology, of body-mind relationships, of thought as a biochemical process, and the effects of drugs on that process. Even Craik's pioneering description of the brain in terms of an electronic model seems quite romantic now in comparison to the factual acceptance of this idea, and of its implications, now. High-boredom Optical art also opens the door to effects that depend on fixation or hypnotic exhaustion of attention. Far from having no content, boredom is a state of potential richness, a desert that is now being irrigated and colonized.

Indeed, insofar as boredom is an absense of climax, it is a well-established entity in modern art. Rauschenberg's work carefully avoids climax or resolution, bringing one back to Merce Cunningham's now classic article on the dancer's movement through a spatial continuum which becomes a substance, a matter defined through the absence of crescendo. In colonizing a climaxless continuum of repetitions the artist is in a way paralleling the repetitive daily fund of experiences of industrial or urban man. Like the experience of urban man, the artist's experience can be stultifying or not, depending on himself.

The robotization of human function has been one of our deepest anxieties since the introduction of the machine. In the mid-sixties, however, the machine has lost that Frankenstein implication, and has become almost amiable in some depictions. (Though in Godard's *Alphaville* (1965) the machine is still considered dangerous and authoritarian—a retrograde view stated with avant-garde means. Robby the benign Robot in *The Forbidden Planet* (1956) is evidence of more realistic thinking.) One of last season's exhibitions, Castro-Cid's, showed ineffectively programmed robots persistently attempting to perform meaningless tasks and sometimes succeeding. In Ernest Trova's work the human figure is reduced to a gleaming armless unit which becomes the main counter in games of repetition and chance.

The robot idea is generally less obvious. But one finds clues to its existence in the unique detachment of what one has been calling high- and low-boredom artists. For the detachment is so complete that it leads again and again to the idea that the work has come not so much from the artist as from his robotized self-image. This substitute ego has a superb ability to handle information fed in for processing and transmission or "expression." Its main characteristics are odd emotional discontinuities and lack of sexual differentiation (in fact, sex in the stand-in self-image may be hysterically transferred or fixated fetishistically). Recently some scientist "artists" in New York (at the Howard Wise Gallery) used real computers as alter egos handling information fed in to create highly sophisticated spatial designs that could be "rotated" into different planes and viewpoints through modifying the formula. In speaking of the alter ego as robot or computer, one is following an old tradition of describing human action through scientific models—modes of action were described in terms of determinist mechanism in the nineteenth century, in terms of psychological models up to a decade ago, and now we find ourselves describing human action in terms of electronics and computer logic, both of which include enough built-in variables to preserve a workable illusion of freedom.

In the relationship between the artist and his hypothetical zombie one can introduce the ideas of acting, role-playing, and substitution. In Abstract Expressionism, as in Method acting, the artist and his role were indivisible. In much mid-sixties art the artist seems to play his role from a safe distance through his zombie, easily providing it with a variety of masks. Obviously this is an arrangement through which sensations can be explored, if not experienced, and through which the multiple confusions of life can be accepted without danger, since there is a built-in isolation.

The same protection applies to the work itself, even though it has been devoured as a commodity by an unprecedented mass audience through TV shows, magazines, and fashion. But the artist's feelings remain hidden except to a few who have learned to read them. So the artist is simultaneously dissociating himself from the public while apparently catering to it. The hidden rage of contradictory feelings under a seemingly blank surface or mask is one of the truest marks of today's art. The language of the mid-sixties can provocatively substitute intention for performance and detachment for aesthetic distance.

How long these ambiguities will remain entrenched in irony it is impossible to say. The undercurrent of irony is evidence of an anarchic strain that has shown itself occasionally in works that seem to be suffering a crise or tantrum of aesthetics by keeping meaning out. On the other hand, the relation of the artist and his phantom self to their environment constitutes a potential situation in which the artistic act can become a sort of primitive social act, a guarded attempt by the artist to move toward the center of his society and to survive there. With this development, the art of the mid-sixties, whatever its exhilarating boredoms, mechanical paradoxes, and emotional discontinuities, has tremendous positive implications. In approaching these implications, the hypotheses of low- and high-boredom art, and the artist's robotized alter ego, are useful.

September 1965
St. Louis Post-Dispatch

A Platonic Academy—Minus Plato:
The Future in New York

THE PRIMARY INTEREST in the coming New York season is undoubtedly in seeing how those in possession of the ball will run with it. The not-so-new object makers (typically they have succeeded in avoiding a catch-phrase title for suitable mass-media marketing) ended last season with something close to total triumph, a dangerous thing to have in a city where current art has tended, since 1962, to mimic the obsolescence of last year's Detroit models.

"Primary Structures: Younger British and American Sculptors" at the Jewish Museum confirmed that position, a position quietly reinforced by "Art in Process," a discriminating show that included the best of the New York contingent. Both exhibitions, coming at the close of the season, gave a tremendous forward impetus to this nonmovement movement instead of ending it—as museum shows here have developed a habit of doing. "The Responsive Eye" at the Modern Museum in 1965 turned out to be the headstone of Op, and the same museum's "Americans 1963" gave Pop a fatal push in the back. (In fact, the Museum of Modern Art is now in the impossible position in which anything it does is wrong—which suggests that public expectations of its role deserve as much clarification as the museum's own interpretation of its position.) But the diffuse, eclectic melange of stripped-down artifacts and artifices, covered by such blanket titles as Primary Structures, Low-Boredom Art, Reductive and Minimal Art, seems to be shunting forward into the new season insulated from obsolescence by certain remarkable new attitudes.

This high-survival quotient, if one can call it that, is due, I think, to an acute estimation of those forces that destroy and discredit new artistic ideas, and the development of a way of coping with these forces. Thus the artists seem to have made a careful study of recent obsolescence cycles, have confronted what has become the illusion of avant-gardism, have developed a sort of intellectual connoisseurship of noncommitment. They have made a diagnosis of the current social situation through which a piece of art is manipulated via the prejudices and indifferences, the expectations and nonexpectations, of the audience; this includes taking into account the habits of museums and collectors, and tickling the hipper-than-thou mass media to pass on the context of ideas in which the new work is seen. It was inevitable that the artist would learn to deal with the so-called "corruptions" that surround the work of art and use them for its survival. The capacity to adapt is, after all, the criterion of survival.

What has emerged instead of a movement is a mode of thinking with certain implicit prescriptions, a mode that projects a kind of mental furniture which has in it the key to survival—for this aesthetic furniture can be all things to all men while remaining totally unchanged. The latest objects, which pretend to be inert or nonemotional (this is simply a brilliant convention of camouflage within which art is functioning now), have clearly patented a way of avoiding all the expectations about how "new" art should behave when it appears. "You are remarkably modern, Mabel," says Lady Markby in An Ideal Husband. "A little too modern, perhaps. Nothing is so dangerous as being too modern. One is apt to grow old-fashioned quite suddenly. I have known many instances of it."

The most intellectually rigorous New York art now (the very best work of such artists as Donald Judd, Robert Smithson, Robert Morris, Robert Grosvenor, among others) cancels the clichés of avant-gardism and sidesteps the expected dialectic. It is through these exact cancellations that the objects are brought into their state of marvelous paralysis, which has reduced some criticism to phenomenology.

Basically these cancellations attack liberal humanism and psychology, on the one hand, and the idea of history on the other. Art is not about life or the "human condition"; it is about art. If art is about "expression" or "feelings," cancel this by producing things which the layman (anyone who doesn't understand a specialty is a layman) is absolved from puzzling over, thus subverting his anxious inquiry with regard to the etiquette of response ("What am I supposed to *feel?*"). If art is about revolution, avoid even counter-revolution. If art is about invention, avoid invention by camouflaging it in an apparent simplicity. If art history is about development, avoid development and subvert scholarship. There are no answers, no problems. Systems fall apart into their components; it is as if all the integers that went into the common denominator had risen above the line. Robbe-Grillet is the theoretician-in-residence. "The world around us turns back into a smooth surface, without signification, without soul, without values, on which we no longer have any purchase. Like the workman who has set down the tool he no longer needs, we find ourselves once again facing *things.*" The gratuitous act is replaced by the gratuitous object. Absurdity, by definition concerned with relationships, is succeeded by a placid contemplation of surfaces which keeps out profundity. Insight is out.

This is seemingly a pretty barren area from which to make art. But it is a great area for just making. Making, however, requires certain models, and since the results are art and thus useless, the models can be as arbitrary as any artist can think of (e.g., solid geometry, bad industrial design, topology, structural engineering, fourth-dimensional paradoxes, etc.). As models, of course, you use them but don't *believe* in them—they are simply the artist's conceptual landscape or "nature." What results from this sort of thing are eclectic inventions which have, as Peter Hutchinson has pointed out, certain Mannerist aspects. But such products are also strongly academic, and the ideas of such "academic" later Mannerists as Lomazzo and Zuccaro, and of course the Carracci, have some limited application if one wishes to follow this as a model for the present.

An academy, strangely enough, is usually concerned with what art cannot be, rather than what it should be. Academic rules, if one reads them in a mirror, deal with what an object is not, rather than what it is. Thus the apparent total permission for artists in New York, which results in forms that look as if they had been passed through an eclectic engine for formal styles and then industrially finished, is not permission at all. It only appears to be so. Painting, figuration, and the textural correlates for memory and nostalgia are proscribed. Also, certain kinds of new materials have become obligatory, and thus other materials have become difficult to use. Dazzled by eclectic possibilities that make concealed invention the subtlest kind of orthodoxy, we have become somewhat blind, in New York, to what the prevalent art has made impossible. And finally, with its strongly anti-avant-garde attitudes, we can speak with confidence of an academy—a new kind of academy that requires more definition, but still an academy. To be avant-garde now is to be old-fashioned.

This academism, far from being the weakness of the present art, is in fact its strength. This art moves into the new season as a conscious academy geared for survival in the lethal New York gallery climate. There are tremendous implications here for the cycle that began, as William Seitz pointed out, with Baudelaire's preface to his Salon of 1846 addressed "To the Bourgeoisie"—the beginning of the split between artist and audience which produced the phenomenon of avant-gardism—is ending. After all, art now, like show jumping, has a reasonably large immediate public, and a vast remote one. The work of art now, smuggling in under its smooth surface the dazzling ideas the layman isn't able to read (and doesn't have to), sits blandly within the gates, announcing that it is not ahead of its time (therefore, arousing no shock), and that the future is simply now. A critic once called Pop "capitalist realism." Perhaps one could call this development "democratic nominalism." This is going to be a tough academy to displace.

This art raises a huge number of questions, and like much modern art is often more interesting to talk about than to look at. The quickest route to the important questions is that this art has apparently no memory and no expectations. It invests itself in multiplying paradoxes, and this excess of paradox leads to stasis. This is the most interesting thing about the current academic structures.

It suggests that one deal with this art not in terms of *facts* (what they are) but in terms of *states* (the conditions that maintain them). Which brings us to areas that will keep coming up in the coming season—the many models which can be applied to illuminate this art; the concepts of time to which this anti-Newtonian art brings us; ideas of scale (this art simply has no scale), and of gravity, which this work contemptuously subverts; the metaphysics of boredom (already a cliché subject); the surface tension of hysteria and mysticism; the supra-illusion with which these works annihilate the dialectic of "reality and illusion"; and the mode in which their creators realize their ideas through third-party technicians who simply carry out the plans. This last does away with any moral bonus the artist gets from working with his hands. Now he works with his mind instead—a scholar-artist whose thoughts are carried out by others. Thus the artist becomes, on the one hand, the draftsman of the environment (on an architectural model); and on the other, an aristocrat like Villiers de l'Isle-Adam's *Axel*: "As for making art? Our technicians will see to that for us." This scholar-philosopher-artist-draftsman-aristocrat leads us to an academy once again, a sort of Platonic Academy—minus Plato.

September 1966
Art and Artists

INDEX